LICHTENBERG'S
VISITS TO ENGLAND

G. Lichtenberg

LICHTENBERG'S VISITS TO ENGLAND

as described in his Letters and Diaries

TRANSLATED AND ANNOTATED

BY

MARGARET L. MARE

AND

W. H. QUARRELL

Lichtenberg, Georg Christoph

BENJAMIN BLOM   New York / London

OXFORD STUDIES
IN MODERN LANGUAGES
AND LITERATURE

General Editor

H. G. FIEDLER

Sometime Taylor Professor of the German Language
and Literature in the University
of Oxford

First Published 1938
Reissued 1969 by
Benjamin Blom, Inc., Bronx, New York 10452
and 56 Doughty Street, London, W.C. 1

Library of Congress Catalog Card Number 71-91906

Printed in the United States of America

PREFACE

MR. MALCOLM LETTS in his *As the Foreigners saw us* (1936) referred to Lichtenberg and said: 'G. C. Lichtenberg still awaits his translator.' Selection is not easy, and the present translation is confined to his letters from England to friends in Germany, a few fragments of his diary, and the articles on the English stage which appeared in the *Deutsches Museum* under the form of letters to H. C. Boie.

In the first edition of Lichtenberg's works, which appeared during the years 1800–5, none of his letters were reproduced. There must, however, have been numbers of them lying in many hands, and in 1825 Dr. Ernst Spangenberg published in Lüneburg seventeen letters (recipient not known), written from Göttingen in 1776, which had been found in Celle by G. H. Spiel, the State Secretary. In his short preface Spangenberg refers to Lichtenberg as *dieser geniale und einzige Denker*. The first representative collection of Lichtenberg's letters appeared in the 1844–6 edition of his works, which was edited by his sons, Georg Christoph, Revenue Director in Hanover, and Christoph Wilhelm, Government Commissary in Oldenburg. Unfortunately filial piety prompted many suppressions and alterations. Another edition, in six volumes, appeared at Göttingen in 1867. During the latter half of the nineteenth century various editors brought further letters to light, but it was not until 1896 that Albert Leitzmann obtained permission from Lichtenberg's grandchildren to go through his literary remains, then in their possession. By this means, and by obtaining the use of a large number of further letters scattered over Germany in many libraries and private collections, A. Leitzmann and C. Schüddekopf, in their edition of Lichtenberg's letters published in 1901, were able to double the number of letters in the 1846 edition and increase that of the 1867 edition also, as well as to restore the original version in many cases.

We specially desire to thank and to acknowledge our debt to the Dieterichsche Verlagsbuchhandlung (founded 1760) of Leipzig, to whom we owe permission to translate and print the letters of 17 April 1770, 8 October 1774, 13 October 1774, 6–17 March 1775, 31 March 1775 (in part), 1 May 1775, 28 September 1775, 13 October 1775, and also permission to use references and extracts in a few others which add to the general interest, and fill in and complete, such as specially the letter of 24 January 1775 to Frau Dieterich.

We also wish to thank both Professor H. G. Fiedler and Miss W. E. Delp of Royal Holloway College for their help in elucidating obscure passages in the original, Dr. R. R. Marett, Rector of Exeter College, for advice on matters of style, and Dr. L. F. Powell for reading the manuscript and giving many useful hints as to annotation.

M. L. M.

W. H. Q.

CONTENTS

INTRODUCTION

GEORG CHRISTOPH LICHTENBERG

Life and Character

LICHTENBERG was born on 1 July 1742, at Oberramstadt, a village near Darmstadt, of which his father Johann Konrad Lichtenberg was the pastor. Georg Christoph was the youngest of a family of eighteen, of whom only one sister and four brothers survived childhood. In 1745 Pastor Lichtenberg was transferred to a parish at Darmstadt, and in 1749 became General Superintendent of the clergy in the district. He was, indeed, one of the higher clergy of Hessen, and came into contact with the court there as the writer of texts both for religious and for secular music in the service of the Landgraf. Although Johann Konrad Lichtenberg died in 1751, when Georg Christoph was only nine years old, the father had time to give a scientific direction to the interests of his youngest son who had inherited much of his own cast of mind. The Pastor was a man of great theological learning, but he delighted in his sermons to make excursions into the realm of science, giving popular expositions of natural phenomena and, above all, of astronomical subjects. During the week his scientific interests found an outlet in giving lessons to his children in mathematics and natural science.

If Lichtenberg resembled his father in the bent of his mind, he owed to his mother the well-balanced outlook and gay temperament which helped him through many adverse circumstances. Jördens[1] describes her as a 'woman of no common kind, of quiet, gentle and virtuous disposition, sympathetic, active and always gay, and happiest when among her own children and in a small circle of chosen friends. She took a peculiar delight in the contemplation of nature: and conversations on the greatness and ordering of the universe and silent glances at the starry heavens

---

[1] K. H. Jördens, *Lexikon deutscher Schriftsteller und Prosaisten*, Leipzig, 1808. 'Eine Frau von nicht gemeiner Art, von sanftem, stillem und tugendhaftem Gemüthe, theilnehmend, thätig und immer heiter, die am liebsten unter ihren Kindern und in einem kleinen Kreise ausgesuchter Freunde lebte. Einen besonderen Reiz für sie hatten Betrachtungen der Natur. Unterhaltungen über die Grösse und Einrichtung des Weltgebäudes und stille Blicke auf den gestirnten Himmel waren für sie Gottesverehrung.'

were for her an adoration of God'. It was well for Lichtenberg
that he had such a mother to help him to rise triumphantly superior to the disability which might otherwise have marred his
whole life. By his eighth year he had become an incurable hunch-
back, owing to a weakness left after a fall caused by the carelessness of a servant. Many years after his mother's death,
Lichtenberg wrote: 'The memory of my mother and her virtue
is like a cordial, which I always take with excellent results, when
I am wavering between good and evil.'[1]

On his father's death Lichtenberg was sent to the Gymnasium
at Darmstadt. Although he excelled in all branches of learning,
even here his scientific bent was apparent, his chief interests being
mathematics, physics, and astronomy. In the latter he included
astrology, being as yet young and credulous. He did his best to
relieve his mother's poverty by coaching some of his fellow-pupils
in mathematics.

In 1763 Lichtenberg received a grant of 400 florins from the
Landgraf of Hessen to enable him to study at the University of
Göttingen. He eked this out with money earned by coaching and
correction of proofs. At this period Göttingen was the most
efficient university in Germany and probably in Europe. The
political connexion between Hanover and England made for freedom of thought, which attracted to Göttingen many extremely able
men, such as Heyne, the founder of classical archaeology (cp.
Letter 1), and Kästner (cp. Letter 2), the physicist and writer of
epigrams, who became Lichtenberg's teacher and lifelong friend.
The equipment was worthy of the personnel of the University.
Mr. Bruford[2] says that ' . . . advanced study and research in history and law, as well as in the mathematical sciences and medicine,
were actively encouraged in Göttingen by the endowment of the
only really satisfactory university library in Germany, together
with scientific and medical laboratories and museums. Göttingen
completed the process, begun at Halle, of bringing the Universities
into touch again with life and attracting the best minds of the day
to their service'. Lichtenberg savoured to the full the stimulating
atmosphere of the place. In spite of the delicacy of his health
and the fact that he had partly to support himself, he found time
to attend lectures in philosophy, history and philology, although

---

[1] Lichtenberg, *Vermischte Schriften* (Göttingen, 1844).
[2] Mr. W. H. Bruford, *Germany in the XVIII Century*, 1935.

by no means neglecting his chief studies of physics and mathematics.

In 1764, his second year at Göttingen, Lichtenberg lost his mother. In addition to this obvious cause for grief, he was at this time probably more acutely aware of his physical disabilities than at any other period. In spite of his frail body he was as full of vitality and natural impulses as any young man of his age, and enjoyed to the full both the intellectual stimulus and the jovial pleasures of student life, so far as his slender purse would allow. But from one pleasure, indulged in freely by his contemporaries, namely that of flirtation, he was largely debarred by his mis-shapen form. It is during this period that Lichtenberg jotted down various reflections, which show him to have toyed with the idea of suicide. For him, however, it was no more than an idea, then fashionable and in the air, which the bed-rock sanity of his nature would never have allowed him to entertain seriously. Through all the contradictions of Lichtenberg's character this sanity runs like a silver thread. There was, indeed, in Lichtenberg a great deal of the hypochondriac. His health was certainly frail, but he is constantly dwelling on and exaggerating his symptoms, as well as inventing many new ones. Unlike most hypochondriacs, however, he was able to observe himself dispassionately and discount his imaginary ills. His reflections are full of trenchant remarks on the subject. Laughing at his own fears, he once said that the doctors only diagnosed one disorder, intestinal cramp, while he himself could perceive the symptoms of thirteen, ranging from *marasmus senilis* to diabetes. Like the modern psychologists he sees clearly: 'My body is that part of the world which my thoughts can affect. Even imagined illnesses may become real ones. But as far as the rest of the world is concerned, my hypotheses cannot upset the order of things.'[1]

In matters of religion, again, there is an apparent contradiction in Lichtenberg's outlook, though this is easily explained by tracing the conflicting elements to their source. Lichtenberg grew up during an age when rationalism was in the air. Hence, like the rest of his contemporaries, he had, by the time he was sixteen, outgrown the belief in the godhead of Christ, though holding firmly to His teaching when cleansed from the 'accursed nonsense of the priests (*verfluchtes Pfaffengeschmiere*)'. Throughout his life

[1] Lichtenberg, op. cit. i. 21.

he professed the current rationalistic opinions of the day. 'As far as the road to Heaven is concerned, all religions are more or less equally good; but our journey on earth, that's the very devil.'[1] His personal religion revealed, however, the ineradicable impress of the parsonage and his share of his mother's mystic leanings. The disciple of tolerance was so deeply imbued with the sturdy protestantism of his home that he could never throw off his prejudice against Roman Catholicism, which he often expressed in a manner somewhat lacking in taste. And yet he indulged in private superstitions of his own, far more irrational than those he attributed to the adherents of the despised religion; though again his saving sense of humour intervenes and makes him aware of the ludicrous contradiction. 'Every movement of a crawling insect gives me the answer to some question about my destiny. Is not this strange in a professor of physics?'[2] The pietism Lichtenberg had inherited from his mother is reflected in countless passages which are strange companions to his rationalistic utterances. The first part of the following extract from *Nachrichten und Bemerkungen des Verfassers über sich selbst* might be pure Werther, though at the end Lichtenberg disclaims any tendency to 'fashionable melancholy':

What a vast difference whether I say these words in my own room or in the immensity of Westminster Abbey: 'Before the mountains were brought forth, or ever the earth and the world were made: Thou art God from everlasting, and world without end.' Above me the solemn vaults, where the sun ever mourns in a dim, religious light; below me the remains of mouldering splendour, the dust of kings; and around me the trophies of death! I have spoken them in both places; in my chamber they have often edified me, and from my childhood I could never repeat them in prayer without emotion; but here I was seized with an indescribable, yet agreeable, sense of awe. I felt the presence of the Judge, whom I could not escape even if I took the wings of the morning, and was moved to tears, fraught neither with sorrow nor joy, but with an inexpressible trust in Him. You who are always conjecturing and reading between the lines, do not think that I am moved by fashionable melancholy to invent this. I did not find it easy to read Young when he was all the mode, and now, when it is the fashion to run him down, I still think him a great man.[3]

Lichtenberg was probably aware of the dual nature of his person-

---

[1] Lichtenberg, op. cit. ii. 87.   [2] Lichtenberg, op. cit. i. 15.
[3] Lichtenberg, op. cit. i. 9.

ality. He was doubtless thinking of himself when he once remarked that man is half spirit and half matter, as a polypus is half
plant and half animal, and that the most curious creatures (*die
seltsamsten Geschöpfe*) are on the boundary line. On another occasion he called Frederick the Great a 'praying freethinker' (*betender
Freigeist*), adding that this was a character often to be found.
Even as a child Lichtenberg managed to combine credulity with
scientific curiosity. He was once known to write on a piece of
paper, 'What is the aurora borealis?' and, addressing it to an
angel, put it in the garret.

The happiest years of Lichtenberg's life were possibly those
which cover the two journeys to England. As soon as he had
completed his studies, he was in great demand as a teacher of
physics, and in 1770 became Professor Extraordinarius at Göttingen, having already refused an offer of a professorship at Giessen,
a university town in his native Hessen. As we have seen, he
enjoyed the society of many distinguished colleagues in the
University, but the craving, always strong in Lichtenberg, for
the delights of family life was satisfied by his friendship with the
Dieterich family. Dieterich was a well-known bookseller and
publisher, a man rather of shrewd common sense than of deep
culture. From Lichtenberg's letters to Herr and Frau Dieterich
it is easy to re-create the atmosphere of their friendly intercourse,
the jokes enjoyed in common and their solicitude for each other's
interests. Dieterich is the one correspondent, outside his own
family, to whom Lichtenberg uses the familiar *du*, and this not
until the letters written on the journey of 1774–5. For the rest of
his life Lichtenberg was never to be far apart from the Dieterich
family; for from his student days onwards he earned house-room,
which increased as the years went on, in their dwelling, in payment for the correction of proofs, and later for editing various
periodicals published by Dieterich.

In matters of general culture, as distinct from science, England
was the dominating influence on Lichtenberg. Being a fluent lin-
guist, he had early mastered enough English to read extensively,
and by 1767 was already a sort of unofficial supervisor to all the
English students in Göttingen. It was in charge of two of these
that he made his first journey to England in 1770, when he stayed
at the house of Lord Boston, the father of Mr. William Irby, one
of these pupils. By him Lichtenberg was presented to George III,

who was much interested in his conversation, especially in an account of the transit of Venus, which Lichtenberg had observed in Kästner's company at Göttingen in the previous year. This interest bore fruit when in 1772 Lichtenberg was commanded by the King to lay aside for the moment his university work, with no loss of salary, however, and to take observations on the latitude and longitude of Hanover, Stade, and Osnabrück. In the course of these observations Lichtenberg enjoyed much pleasant intercourse with official circles in Hanover and took the opportunity, when in Stade, of making an enterprising voyage of discovery to Heligoland. It was to report on this work to George III, and also to lay before him the writings of Tobias Mayer which he had just finished editing (cp. Letter 8), that Lichtenberg undertook his second journey to England in September 1774. On this occasion he stayed over a year, and came into contact with all sorts and conditions of Englishmen. 'When I was in England, I lived sometimes like a lord and at others like a workman,' he writes. He became well acquainted with such men as Banks, Solander, and the two Forsters, and gained an intimate knowledge of English society, where he was widely introduced by his aristocratic pupils. His innate sympathy for all things English made him acceptable to every one he met. So well was he liked, indeed, by the Irby brothers that they insisted on Lichtenberg's remaining with their father, Lord Boston, all through his last illness.

On his return to Göttingen in 1775 Lichtenberg was appointed Professor Ordinarius in that university. After five years of change and distraction, he settled down there for the remaining twenty-four years of his life, leaving Göttingen only for short journeys to Hamburg or Gotha. Lichtenberg was probably the most sought-after professor in the University. At least eighty or a hundred students attended his lectures, while it frequently happened that he had to turn many away for lack of room. He was in advance of his contemporaries in providing facilities for more experimental work in physics than was usual at the period. He also lectured on mathematics and astronomy. In 1785 Lichtenberg's fame as a scientist brought him the three youngest sons of George III, who had been sent to Göttingen to finish their education, as private pupils in physics. After this further proof of the esteem felt for him by the royal house, he received the title of Hofrat.

Lichtenberg married late in life. It is obvious from the frequent

allusions in the letters to Dieterich that he was far from indifferent to pretty girls, and it was perhaps the saddest aspect
of his physical affliction that his bodily charms fell so far short of
the whimsical mind and kindly nature, which would have endeared
him to women of the most fastidious taste. With Lichtenberg
nature would not be denied, and from his student days onwards
he had to content himself with a series of passing love affairs, such
as his purse and his attractions permitted. The bed-makers who
attended on the students of Göttingen were often fresh-looking
country girls from the valleys of the Harz, and Lichtenberg once
remarked that he preferred these naïve creatures to the profes-
sional harpies, with their brooches and feathered hats. But as
middle age approached, he felt the need of some more permanent
liaison. The story of his first attempt to satisfy this desire reads
like a novel. One day in 1777 Lichtenberg was taking a walk along
the ramparts with some of his English pupils, when they came on
a girl of twelve or thirteen selling flowers. 'God Almighty, what
a handsome girl,' remarked one of the young men. As Lichtenberg
wrote later to one of his friends, he made inquiries about her, being
apprehensive as to what might be her fate in 'such a Sodom as
Göttingen'. She turned out to be Maria Dorothea Stechard, the
daughter of a weaver in the city. Lichtenberg arranged with her
mother to have her every day at his house, where she performed
useful household tasks and received lessons from him in writing
and arithmetic and other small accomplishments. She loved the
shining metal of his scientific apparatus, and enjoyed playing with
and cleaning it, just as much as looking after her benefactor's
cravats. After a time Maria became Lichtenberg's mistress, and
so endeared herself to him that he had made up his mind to marry
her, when she died suddenly of a fever, just after she had turned
seventeen.

Not long after Maria's death Lichtenberg consoled himself with
another mistress, Margarethe Kellner, a pretty girl who used to
go about the town selling fruit. Very little is known of her. She
was born on 31 August 1759 at Nikolausberg near Göttingen, and
died in 1848 at the great age of 89. As early as 1784 Lichtenberg
speaks in a letter of Margarethe as 'meine Frau', but he did not
marry her legally until October 1789, after the birth of several of
their eight children. Of these two died in infancy, three sons and
three daughters surviving their father. Most of those who have

written biographical notices on Lichtenberg speak as though it
was entirely owing to his deformity that he had to be content with
a woman of the people, *faute de mieux*. We have only to think,
however, of the greatest of his contemporaries to realize that such
a union could satisfy a man both of handsome person and brilliant
intellect. Goethe had deserted a Friederike and acquiesced in
parting with a Lili, to find happiness with a Christiane Vulpius.
Lichtenberg was probably at heart more inclined to good bourgeois domesticity than was Goethe. His eulogies of the family life
of King George and Queen Charlotte, and his report on the
King's views on the expediency of marriage (cp. Letter 10), ring
true, and might well come from the pen of Fanny Burney of
whom it was said, 'Poor Fan is such a prude'. Lichtenberg was
obviously one of those men who are content to rest from their
intellectual labours by the side of a partner who can have no share
in them. He and his wife were perfectly happy. She nursed him
devotedly in sickness, and was his bright and cheerful companion
when he was in health. They never quarrelled, except in fun,
when they would argue with as much wit as each could muster,
doing this, as Lichtenberg wrote in his diary, so that if either of
them ever married again, they would not be out of practice.
Lichtenberg was devoted to children; so, in providing him with
a quiverful, in this respect too Margarethe did her duty. In a letter
to one of his friends Lichtenberg once remarked that rather
than have a wife who gave him no children, he would as soon have
a wife in a painting, or fall in love with the Mother of God (*mich
in die Muttergottes verlieben*).[1]

While Margarethe was still Lichtenberg's mistress, polite society
appears to have been content to ignore her and to open its arms to
her lover. After the legal marriage, however, it withdrew, shocked
at the *mésalliance*. The Lichtenberg we see in the English letters,
being in his most sociable mood, might well have been hurt by this,
though even at this period he hints now and then at a longing for
solitude in the midst of the distractions of life in London. But by
the 1790's Lichtenberg had come to find his best company in the
resources of his own mind. His only grief was the estrangement
from his brother, Ludwig Christian, who, in disgust at Lichtenberg's low marriage, left off writing to him for some years. With
increasing bodily infirmities he often kept the house for months on

[1] Letter to Semmering, 20 April 1791.

end, though pupils and friends frequently broke in on his solitude. All the change he needed was provided by visits to the little house on the Weender Strasse, just outside the town, which he took in 1790. The ever-faithful Dieterich would take him out there and bring him back in his carriage. In spring and autumn Lichtenberg spent his free days sitting in the charming garden of his house, enjoying his flowers and the songs of the birds. When his mood was one of melancholy reflection, he enjoyed gazing on his future grave in the cemetery near by, or whistling one of his favourite chorales. The pleasures of his life in these latter years were playing with the children, moderate wine-drinking, smoking, and snuff-taking. Like the royal mistress he admired so heartily, he enjoyed his snuff without restraint, getting through a pound a week.

In these years Lichtenberg's interests were focused less and less on literature, and more exclusively on scientific subjects. In science his work was original, and his discovery in electricity of the so-called 'Lichtenberg figures' is still recognized by scientists as important. In his diary he notes the middle of the year 1791 as being the turning-point when his scientific interests got the upper hand. He remarks that he is filled with distrust of all human knowledge, with the exception of mathematics. What chains him to the study of physics is 'the hope of discovering something of value to the human race' ('die Hoffnung, etwas dem menschlichen Geschlechte Nützliches aufzufinden'). Thus he lived and worked, actuated by the unselfish spirit of true scientific research, until he died, after a short attack of pneumonia, on 18 February 1799, at the age of 56 years 8 months.

England and Hanover

In his introduction to *Briefe aus Lichtenbergs englischem Freundeskreis* (Göttingen, 1925) Hans Hecht remarks that, in connexion with Lichtenberg, there arises 'die weitere Aufgabe einer Darstellung der Beziehungen der hannoverischen Landesuniversität zu England, sowohl als empfangende wie als spendende Kraftquelle und erheblicher Faktor bei der Betrachtung der Entwicklung deutschen Geisteslebens in der zweiten Hälfte des achtzehnten Jahrhunderts'.[1] It is indeed true that this aspect of Lichtenberg has been quickly disposed of by those who have hitherto written

[1] 'The further task of describing the relations of the Hanoverian State

about him. We have, therefore, in the present translation confined ourselves to Lichtenberg's letters from England, in order to provide material for the consideration of this most interesting subject.

Germany in the eighteenth century was a collection of small states, whose rulers had it in their power to be either a 'Landesvater' or a tyrant. Their character was all-important to their subjects, and often the only hope of getting justice under an autocratic government was to attend the daily audiences held by these rulers. Lichtenberg followed this precedent when he handed over the petition of his friend Dieterich to George III (Letter 20). The disadvantages of an absentee Elector are made clear by Lichtenberg's remarks to Heyne in his letter of 6 March 1775, as to the course taken by the royal bounty in its passage from England to Hanover, a stream 'abundant and pure' at the source being apt to dwindle away into 'a few muddied drops'.

The first two Georges had never allowed their English subjects to forget that they were Electors of Hanover, a land from which they felt themselves to be to some extent exiles, in spite of the ample compensation of the revenues of their new kingdom. But when we consider the English-born George III, we are apt to lose sight of the fact that he was responsible for the welfare of German as well as English subjects; and we realize with a start of surprise that Lichtenberg owed allegiance to the same ruler as his English friends acknowledged. His letters from England throw an interesting light on George's and Charlotte's methods of keeping in touch with their Hanoverian subjects. A shrewd commentator such as Lichtenberg, too honest to be servile, must have been a godsend to the royal couple. Through his eyes we see them at their best. To fashionable society, for the most part, their domestic virtue appeared humdrum, but the bourgeois world, whether German or English, thought it charming. Lichtenberg concurs with other middle-class reporters, such as Fanny Burney, in this respect. To him, however, they probably appeared more intelligent than to the English Miss Burney. The Queen, at any rate, would be more at home in discussing literary matters in her native tongue. We see her lending to Lichtenberg Lavater's latest work, at that time the talk of cultured circles in Germany (Letter 18).

University with England, as a source both for the reception and transmission of energy, and an important factor in considering the development of intellectual life in Germany during the second half of the eighteenth century.'

George III welcomed in Lichtenberg a member of the University of Göttingen, whose welfare he had at heart and of which he was an enlightened patron, and delighted in hearing from him of all that was going on there. Lichtenberg was certainly a more seemly representative of the academic world than those Oxford dons described by Miss Burney, who 'the moment they had kissed the King's hand, turned their backs on him, and walked away as in any common room . . . and many, in their confusion, fairly arose by pulling his Majesty's hand to raise them'. It is hardly surprising that George III's sons finished their education at Göttingen rather than at an English University.

Hanover was said to be the best governed state in Germany at this period, not even excepting the Prussia of Frederick the Great. 'In Hanover, in the absence of the Electors . . . the nobility maintained an oligarchical rule through the Estates . . . but, though they ruled in their own interests, there was at least no extravagant court to be maintained, the English connexion made for freedom of thought, and the people were comparatively contented.'[1] The press was for these reasons more free than in the other German states. In spite of all this, Lichtenberg is constantly harping on the superiority of English institutions. Comparatively free as Hanover might be, England was the land of freedom itself. When Lichtenberg was in England, the American storm had not yet broken, though angry clouds were piled up on the horizon. Professor G. M. Trevelyan writes that at the beginning of George III's reign England 'was held in higher esteem by the nations of the world than ever before or since'. This was still true, and even a Parliament where the 'King's friends' held sway was a unique institution. As Lichtenberg remarked, in England liberty was assured by the constitution, while in Hanover it depended on the benevolence of the King.

In matters of lesser moment, too, England was more civilized than the German states. Almost incredible as it may seem nowadays, English inns were superior to continental ones, as most travellers affirm. In his account of his foreign travels in 1772, Dr. Burney remarks that 'the excellent roads, inns and carriages throughout Great Britain make an Englishman very unfit to encounter such hardships'. It is easier to believe in the superiority of our roads. We are on the threshold of the period when young

[1] Bruford, op. cit.

bucks of the Regency were to race for wagers along the Brighton road in their curricles, while in Germany one was liable to breakdowns, such as Lichtenberg experienced in 1770 on the road from Osnabrück (Letter 2).

Perhaps the greatest advantage English society had over that of Germany in the eighteenth century was the greater fluidity of the classes. In Germany there was a great gulf fixed between the aristocracy and middle classes. How deep it was may well be seen from the difficulties encountered by the bourgeois Goethe, before he could be admitted to the magic circle that played cards with Herzogin Luise, the wife of the Duke of Weimar. In Germany a Mrs. Thrale become Mrs. Piozzi could never have won her way back even into the outworks of society. A Garrick or a Joshua Reynolds, however great his talents, would have belonged to a caste apart. Lichtenberg does not expressly make such comparisons, but the letters, describing his reception in English society, would speak for themselves to his German friends. The German aristocracy, divorced from stimulating contact with the highly educated element in the middle classes, was cut off, for the most part, from the development of native thought and owed such culture as it had largely to French inspiration. In England society was willing to bow down to the literary dictation of a Dr. Johnson.

It is not surprising that Lichtenberg received a great stimulus from his contact with English life, and had frequently to be twitted with his Anglomania. There was, indeed, a similarity between his cast of mind and our own, which made him all the more receptive of impressions. English thought is usually based on practical psychology and observation of human nature. Lichtenberg was acute enough to perceive this common denominator in Shakespeare and in Garrick as his interpreter, while he saw in Hogarth's paintings another expression of Pope's axiom concerning the proper study of mankind. His philosophical ideas do not hover in the empyrean, as do those of the typical German philosopher, but are rather based on study of the earth and its inhabitants.

Lichtenberg and German literature

'If I could but make canals in my head in order to expedite inland trade between my stores of ideas! But there they lie in hundreds, without being of the least use to each other.'[1] In these words Lichtenberg puts in a nutshell the reason why he failed to achieve a more impressive place in the history of German literature. The versatility of his genius and the wideness of his interests prevented him from devoting himself to one particular form of art and excelling in it. He no doubt thought of himself primarily as a physicist, and considered literature as the sport of the moment, or as a means of bringing grist to the mill.

Hitherto Lichtenberg's aphorisms have received more consideration from students of literature than his other works. We do not propose here to examine his position as a philosopher. It is sufficient to remark that Schopenhauer, who admired him for the originality and independence of his thought, counted Lichtenberg among his favourite authors, while he was much read by Nietzsche and Richard Wagner, and even reached as far afield as to Tolstoi. It is interesting to note that Kant, who had so much influence on the thought of the mature Lichtenberg, possessed a well-thumbed copy of the *Aphorisms*, in which he underlined the satirical rather than the philosophical utterances. The *Aphorisms* are, indeed, jottings, such as one would expect from a brilliant man living in an age when it was the fashion to diarize one's intimate feelings and reflections. They are full of original ideas and trenchant humour, and have as their coping-stone a wide and penetrating knowledge of human nature.

Lichtenberg wrote many pamphlets of a polemical nature which cannot have any great interest for posterity, though at the time they achieved their object. Ill-advised critics have attempted to compare his satire with that of Swift, though there is little in common between the undiluted vitriol of the great Dean and the utterances, sharp only to the point of mild stimulation, of the lesser man.

Here we are concerned with Lichtenberg as an interpreter of every branch of English art. Bound up with this is his opinion of the productions of his own fellow countrymen. Lichtenberg was a born dramatic critic. The enthusiastic but shrewd comments on Garrick contained in the Letters to Boie are amazing, when one reflects that the author was a veritable 'country cousin', as far as theatre-going was concerned, and had probably only seen first-class acting when on visits to Hanover. His articles enjoyed a

[1] Lichtenberg, op. cit. i. 23.

wide circulation in Boie's *Deutsches Museum*, and were much talked of as being the only authentic German description of the interpretation of Shakespeare on the stage of his native land. For the last ten years or so Lessing had been holding up Shakespeare as a model for German imitation, but neither he nor Wieland, who was the first to make a German translation of Shakespeare's works, had ever been in England. It was work such as Lichtenberg's that paved the way for that great feat of translation, the Schlegel Shakespeare. One may even imagine that, when A. W. Schlegel was studying at Göttingen under Heyne, he met Lichtenberg, and entered with him into enthusiastic discussion of the world's greatest dramatist.

Some of Lichtenberg's critics appear surprised that he did not, in common with a large section of the public, on the production of *Götz von Berlichingen*, see in Goethe a rising German Shakespeare. The very comparison, indeed, seemed to Lichtenberg impious; so that he once remarked that it was as likely *Götz* would be played at Drury Lane as that the King of England should be elected by the cardinals at St. Peter's. He was rendered even more critical of the play by the spate of imitations, each one worse than the last; and in the course of the letters to Boie, he indulges in a good many hits at these 'would-be geniuses'. Lichtenberg has been accused of lack of fairness to Goethe, because *Götz* and *Werther* were not to his taste, but such critics forget his appreciation of *Wilhelm Meister*, and the fact that he did not live to know some of Goethe's greatest work. He was, moreover, forced in his correspondence with Goethe over the *Farbenlehre* into a very non-committal attitude, being as a conscientious scientist unable to congratulate him on a work based on what he deemed to be a fallacy. Goethe's greatest works known to Lichtenberg were, probably, his earlier lyrics, and for lyric poetry Lichtenberg lacked really deep feeling.

In his criticism both of the 'Sturm und Drang' poets and the 'Göttinger Hainbund' Lichtenberg was, perhaps, over-severe, though posterity endorses most of his views. It is true that he refused to see the better qualities of *Werther*, and was inclined to swell the army of the parodists of that work (Letter 15). In fact, he planned to write *Parakletor*, a satire on the whole of the 'Sturm und Drang' poets, though, perhaps fortunately, the work never got beyond a few tentative jottings. Many of the remarks which might

have gone to make up such a work are brilliant, as for instance
that 'The German is never more of an imitator than when he
wants to be absolutely original'. As for the 'Hainbund' (cp. Letters
9 PS. and 11), their lack of appreciation for Wieland set Lichtenberg against them, though much of his criticism is justified. The
fact that this coterie of second-rate poets idolized Klopstock made
Lichtenberg somewhat blind to his merits. He once rather un-
fairly remarked that he would give the *Messias* twice over for a
small part of *Robinson Crusoe*.

In other cases Lichtenberg's judgement on his contemporaries
is admirable. He was never carried along by the stream of adula-
tion of the specious Lavater, but wrote many polemics against his
phrenological theories. It was while in England that Lichtenberg
had his first sight of the *Physiognomische Fragmente*, Queen Charlotte having lent the book to him (Letter 18). Lichtenberg's real
affinity was with men of reason, such as Lessing, so that he does
full justice to Lessing's greatness. He also appreciated the writings
of Nicolai and his coterie.

Lichtenberg was convinced of the superiority of English to
German literature, and he never let slip an opportunity of ex-
pounding the beauties of his favourite authors—Shakespeare,
Pope, Swift, Fielding, Sterne. He perhaps knew more of English
literature than any other German of his period. As a Shakespeare
critic he dwells more on the psychologist and dramatist than on
the poet, though this was the case, indeed, with many of his contemporaries, even in England. In all his appreciations of English
authors, he is constantly stressing their good sense and patient
study of mankind, and contrasting it with what he conceives to
be the German defect of waiting on inspiration.

As widely read in Germany at the time they appeared as his
letters to Boie were Lichtenberg's explanations of Hogarth's engravings, which were published from 1794 onwards. He admitted
in a letter to Goethe that they were hack work, undertaken at a
time when his family was becoming large and expensive; but even
the sense that he was working at a task could not obscure his
appreciation of Hogarth as a typical example of English genius.
Lichtenberg's elucidations are more valuable for the sidelights
thrown on English life and character than as criticisms of art.

In view of the enormous volume of Lichtenberg's output,
spread out over the many literary periodicals of the day, and the

countless books of diaries and aphorisms, it is amazing that he does not more frequently decline into a slipshod manner. His style is, indeed, natural and unaffected and, despite its allusiveness, not over-elaborate. He confesses to a love of comparisons and images to express his thoughts,[1] and on the whole they embellish rather than obscure his diction. They are not easy to reproduce in an English translation.

When we consider that Lichtenberg is worthy of notice in histories of the development of science, of philosophy, and of literature, and that here we have been able to fill a book by taking yet another aspect of his work, his versatility is borne in on us. In the introduction to his edition of Lichtenberg's *Aphorisms*, Leitzmann has called him the 'modernsten Geist des 18. Jahrhunderts'. In some respects this may be so, but as regards our modern trend towards specialization it is far from true. Lichtenberg described his manifold activities in his own whimsical manner when he said: 'Ich habe den Weg zur Wissenschaft gemacht wie die Hunde, die mit ihrem Herrn spazieren gehen: hundertmal denselben vorwärts und rückwärts, und als ich ankam, war ich müde.'[2]

M. L. M.

---

[1] Lichtenberg, op. cit. i. 19.
[2] Ibid. 'I have followed the path of knowledge like a dog going for a walk with its master; running to and fro a hundred times; so that, when I arrived, I was weary.'

LETTERS FROM ENGLAND

being articles which appeared in the DEUTSCHES
MUSEUM[1] *in 1776 and 1778, addressed to the Editor,*
HEINRICH CHRISTIAN BOIE

I

London, 1 October 1775.

I can now, my dear B.,[2] comply, I hope, better with your request
to write you some account of Mr. Garrick than when first you
made it. At that time I had seen this extraordinary man but
twice; this was not long enough to observe him quietly, and the
time was too short to allow me to write of it to a friend at my
leisure. I now send you a few of my notes; not all of them, but
you shall have the rest later, if you wish; observations and arguments pell-mell and probably more digressions than both put
together; everything told as plainly as possible, that is to say, in
the order and with the expressions dictated by the mood of the
moment at which I am writing. Pray excuse me, for I am loath
to set about letters where I may not do this, and, indeed, I would
rather put off writing them until the next day—and then for ever.
Let me add that, although there is no style, short of utter nonsense,
I detest more than the solemn, portentous Boswellian tone
whereby many authors exalt any great man whom they are
appraising into an angel and the writer himself into a prophet,
stammering forth a certain ornate prose such as vastly magnifies
the truth, nevertheless it may be (though I hope not) that my
subject has played that very trick on me. If you notice any such

[1] See Appendix, p. 123, for note on 'The *Deutsches Museum* and its place
among German Literary Periodicals in the eighteenth century'.

[2] Heinrich Christian Boie was born in 1744 at Meldorf in Ditmarschen, of
which his father was pastor. He was educated at the Gelehrtenschule at Flens-
burg and at the Universities of Jena and Göttingen. After living precariously
by private tutoring and literary work, he became in 1776 Second Staff Secretary
to the Commander-in-Chief of the Hanoverian Army, and in 1781 Landvogt
of Lüdditmarschen. He married, first, in 1785 Luise Mejer, and, after her death
in 1786, as his second wife, in 1788, Sara von Hugo, by whom he had five
children. He died at Meldorf in 1806. Boie was the author of several original
poems, but most of these are forgotten, with the exception of the student song,
'Die Lore am Tore', based on Henry Carey's 'Sally in our Alley'. He is remembered chiefly as one of the great editors of the literary periodicals of his day (see
note above).

thing, my friend, pray discount it yourself, thanking me, moreover, for not writing to you in my first ardour.

By this time I have seen Mr. Garrick play eight times, frequently in some of his most remarkable parts. Once as Abel
Drugger in Ben Jonson's *Alchemist*, which was much altered;
once as Archer in Farquhar's *Stratagem*; once as Sir John Brute
in Vanbrugh's *Provoked Wife*; twice as Hamlet; once as Lusignan
in *Zaïre*, adapted by Hill;[1] once as Benedick in Shakespeare's
Much Ado About Nothing, and finally as Don Leon in Beaumont
and Fletcher's *Rule a Wife and have a Wife*. I have, moreover,
conversed with him and, what is more, have been made free of
his box.

Among the characters I have mentioned they say that Weston[2]
equals him as Abel Drugger, as did Quin[3] formerly as Sir John
Brute; but as yet no man has set foot on the British stage who is
his equal in the other parts; moreover, there is no one who can
hope to come up to such a man in any one part, still less to play
them all with the same ease. I should fancy, too, that any comparison with Quin and Weston is made with due reservation.
I was not able, indeed, to see Quin as Sir John Brute, and I have
not yet seen Weston as Abel Drugger; but similar pronouncements
on Garrick—and this, indeed, in parts where I could compare
them—have rendered me very sceptical. I am, rather, more or
less convinced that in parts that he has once taken no one may
absolutely surpass him who is not a Garrick, with soul and body
permeated with histrionic talent; and England has never seen on
its stage another such man. I must explain to you what bearing
the opinion of those persons of Weston and Quin has on the matter,
at the same time telling you much concerning Mr. Garrick that
I might otherwise have forgotten; moreover, I should not like you
to conclude from all that I have said that I do not like Weston,
a man at present the idol of the people, who made me laugh more
than all the rest of the English players together. Later I will tell
you more about him, but for the present the following will serve
my purpose.

Weston is one of the drollest creatures on whom I have ever

---

[1] Aaron Hill, 1685–1750, the dramatist.

[2] Thomas Weston, 1737–76, a well-known actor, the son of a cook in the
kitchen of George II. Abel Drugger was one of his finest parts.

[3] James Quin, the celebrated actor, 1693–1766.

set eyes. Figure, voice, demeanour and all about him move one
to laughter, although he never seems to desire this and himself
never laughs. Scarcely has he appeared on the stage than a large
part of the audience becomes oblivious of the play and heeds
nothing but him and his antics. You see, then, that before such
judges a man like this cannot play badly. People have eyes for
him alone. With Garrick it is quite otherwise, for one perpetually
sees him as an effective part of the whole and a faithful mirror of
nature. Therefore he could play his part badly in the eyes of his
England, while Weston could scarce do so. Now Ben Jonson has
indicated only a few points in Abel Drugger's character; and if
a player can once get his line from this, he can proceed more or
less *à son aise* with no fear of overstepping the mark. Weston has
an excellent opportunity of ridding himself of his own personality,
especially in the long intervals when Abel Drugger is dumb and
in a room where there are, besides a few astronomers and exor-
cisers, human skeletons, crocodiles, ostrich eggs and empty
vessels, in which the devil himself could sit. I can almost see him,
rigid with terror at every violent movement of the astrologer or
at the least noise of which the cause is not apparent, standing
like a mummy with feet together; only when it is over does life
return to his eyes and he looks about him, then turns his head
round slowly, and so forth. Most of the audience clap and laugh,
and even the critic smiles at the ridiculous fellow. But when
Garrick plays Abel Drugger it is the critic who leads the applause.
Here we have a vastly different creature, an epitome of the
author's purpose, heightened by a comprehensive knowledge of
his characteristic traits, and interpreted so that he may be clearly
understood from the top gallery downwards. He does not lack
the language of gesture, if I may so express it, in an indolent all-
embracing torpidity, which finally, indeed, becomes unnatural;
but every moment poor Abel is giving fresh indications of his
character; superstition and simplicity. I only mention one
feature, which Mr. Weston could not even imitate and assuredly
could not have invented, and of which I do not suppose the author
himself had thought. When the astrologers spell out from the
stars the name, Abel Drugger, henceforth to be great, the poor
gullible creature says with heartfelt delight: 'That is my name.'
Garrick makes him keep his joy to himself, for to blurt it out
before every one would be lacking in decency. So Garrick turns

aside, hugging his delight to himself for a few moments, so that he actually gets those red rings round his eyes which often accompany great joy, at least when violently suppressed, and says to himself: 'That is my name.' The effect of this judicious restraint is indescribable, for one did not see him merely as a simpleton being gulled, but as a much more ridiculous creature, with an air of secret triumph, thinking himself the slyest of rogues. Nothing like this can be expected of Weston. But when his own particular simplicity of demeanour suits the play, he does wonders, as, for instance, when he plays Dr. Last in Foote's *Devil upon two Sticks*, or Mawworm in *The Hypocrite*, or Scrub in *The Stratagem*. I have seen him in all three parts; in the latter he plays some scenes with Garrick. I think, my dear B., that these scenes would bring puckers of mundane laughter even to ——'s cheeks, which have long been set in a mould of canting piety that the things of this world cannot shake.

Quin's Sir John Brute is, I fancy, a parallel case. The persons who thought him Garrick's equal (one or two of them even preferred him) in this part added that Quin himself had been a kind of Sir John; which made me at least unwilling to place much confidence in their judgement. A man needs strength to play a weak creature well on the stage, and knowledge of polite society and the value of good manners to represent the drunken, debauched Sir John, at least before persons of quality and taste. There are, unfortunately, Sir Johns in all walks of life: thus Quin, I fancy, played a good-for-nothing sportsman to please the fox-hunters, country squires, and braggarts; while Garrick played the wastrel of birth and breeding for the court and persons of taste. It cannot be denied, of course, that an actor can often do this without injustice to the author. What a vast difference there is, for example, between a slow, drawling 'the . . . take me', spoken in the woods with a heavy pipe hanging out of the mouth, and the same words tripping, like some swift ejaculation, off a pair of pretty lips at the billiard-table or on the parade. Moreover, great changes have been made in the play itself. I should also mention that while, on the one hand, Garrick's enemies hold Quin to be his equal, because he has really been a Sir John Brute, on the other I have heard them cast aspersions on Garrick's character because he plays Sir John Brute so well. I have even read this latter statement in a public newspaper. So you see that every day Garrick still meets with

'Partridges'.[1] So now from all these instances you can easily draw your own conclusions as to what they mean by—'Weston and Quin equal Garrick', without any need of a summing up from me. One faction reckons the value of a comic actor by the degree in which he tickles their fancy, without asking whether he achieves this as a player by outstanding excellence in his part, or as a clown, whose tricks have no connexion with it; the other, from lack of taste or knowledge of the world, demands exaggerated characteristics and finds what it wants in the so-called natural style or even in the affected. Such people would often like absolutely to criticize Garrick, if they could do so with impunity; but they would be risking their credit too far, so their bad taste and lack of experience find expression but occasionally, when they maintain a worse player to be his equal. I admit (and who will not?) that thousands cannot see all that Garrick has to show them, for in this respect he is not a whit more fortunate than those congenial spirits, Shakespeare and Hogarth. In order to miss nothing of their art, one must bring one's own little light to eke out the usual illumination.

What is it, then, which gives this man so great a superiority? There are very many causes for it, my friend, and a large proportion of them may be ascribed to the vastly fortunate shape of the man. But, notwithstanding I have been entirely carried away by its effect, I do not dare to analyse it in every given case. For this purpose one requires greater knowledge of the world and more practice in this analysis and opportunities of comparison than I have had. In the meantime, since many things are made unexpectedly clear by intercourse with persons of various rank, habits, and demeanour (a vast deal has become clearer to me than it was in the beginning), and because I can always see the form and face of the man in his chief parts, as if he were before me in the flesh, I shall perhaps in the future, when I am with you again, be able to give you a more coherent account of him. For the moment you must piece it together for yourself from my letters. I have been told that a man here is at work on a treatise for actors[2] which is to

[1] A reference to the character of Mr. Partridge in *Tom Jones*.
[2] Lichtenberg may possibly be referring to *The Elements of Dramatic Criticism*, by William Cooke (London, 1775). The dedication of the book is to Garrick and begins thus: 'As every subject which leads to the further elucidation of the drama necessarily claims the protection of its ablest *practical commentator*, I shall make no apology for inscribing this book to you . . .'

contain rules deduced from Garrick, but by philosophical methods reduced to first principles and rendered connected and clear. I have heard no more of the matter. But if it be so, Heaven send that the man be a Lessing,[1] of whom there are, alas, as few here as in Germany. They said he was a young man, which made me apprehensive; for here, as in Germany, there abound young would-be geniuses, as they term themselves, full of original ideas, who never let slip an opportunity of bringing out their immature and ill-expressed notions, to the delight of their youthful and senti-mental admirers, but to the disgust of the real thinker, who does not absorb a single drop of nourishment from their torrents of Olympian prose. And now, to the point.

There is in Mr. Garrick's whole figure, movements, and pro-priety of demeanour something which I have met with rarely in the few Frenchmen I have seen and never, except in this instance, among the large number of Englishmen with whom I am ac-quainted. I mean in this context Frenchmen who have at least reached middle age; and, naturally, those moving in good society. For example, when he turns to some one with a bow, it is not merely that the head, the shoulders, the feet and arms, are engaged in this exercise, but that each member helps with great propriety to produce the demeanour most pleasing and appropriate to the occasion. When he steps on to the boards, even when not express-ing fear, hope, suspicion, or any other passion, the eyes of all are immediately drawn to him alone; he moves to and fro among other players like a man among marionettes. From this no one, indeed, will recognize Mr. Garrick's ease of manner, who has never re-marked the demeanour of a well-bred Frenchman, but, this being the case, this hint would be the best description. Perhaps the following will make the matter clearer. His stature is rather low than of middle height, and his body thickset. His limbs are in the most pleasing proportion, and the whole man is put together most charmingly. Even the eye of the connoisseur cannot remark any defect either in his limbs, in the manner they are knit, or in his movements. In the latter one is enchanted to observe the fullness of his strength, which, when shown to advantage, is more pleasing than extravagant gestures. With him there is no rampaging, gliding, or slouching, and where other players in the movements

[1] Gotthold Ephraim Lessing, 1729–81, the great critic and dramatist (cf. Appendix, p. 123).

of their arms and legs allow themselves six inches or more scope in every direction farther than the canons of beauty would permit, he hits the mark with admirable certainty and firmness. It is therefore refreshing to see his manner of walking, shrugging his shoulders, putting his hands in his pockets, putting on his hat, now pulling it down over his eyes and then pushing it sideways off his forehead, all this with so slight a movement of his limbs as though each were his right hand. It gives one a sense of freedom and well-being to observe the strength and certainty of his movements and what complete command he has over the muscles of his body. I am convinced that his thickset form does much towards producing this effect. His shapely legs become gradually thinner from the powerful thighs downwards, until they end in the neatest foot you can imagine; in the same way his large arms taper into a little hand. How imposing the effect of this must be you can well imagine. But this strength is not merely illusory. He is really strong and amazingly dexterous and nimble. In the scene in *The Alchemist* where he boxes, he runs about and skips from one neat leg to the other with such admirable lightness that one would dare swear that he was floating in the air. In the dance in *Much Ado about Nothing*, also, he excels all the rest by the agility of his springs; when I saw him in this dance, the audience was so much delighted with it that they had the impudence to cry *encore* to their Roscius. In his face all can observe, without any great refinement of feature, the happy intellect in his unruffled brow, and the alert observer and wit in the lively eye, often bright with roguishness. His gestures are so clear and vivacious as to arouse in one similar emotions. With him one looks serious, with him one wrinkles one's forehead, and with him one smiles; in his intimate joy and the friendly manner in which he appears in an aside to take the audience into his confidence, there is something so insinuating that one's heart goes out to this charming man.

You have probably already heard in Germany, as I did, of his gift for changing his expression. The enthusiasm both of his compatriots and of travellers tends, I expect, to cause some exaggeration, but I dare swear that more than half is true, a tolerably reasonable estimate for enthusiasts. Mr. Garrick has, in truth, attained to an amazing proficiency in it. I will give you examples of this, when I describe him in his different parts; here I will only mention that my attention was drawn to his mouth immediately he came on the stage as Sir John Brute, when I could get a near view of him. He had let it droop somewhat at both corners, which gave him an amazingly dissolute and drunken air. He maintained this expression right up to the end, varying it only by letting his mouth fall open as he became more intoxicated; this expression must be so closely associated in the man's mind with his idea of Sir John Brute, that it is produced without premeditation, or otherwise he would forget to put it on in the midst of all the noise, of which, indeed, he makes not a little in this play.

Now, pray consider further: after having been a law student, this man, of excellent parts and endowed by nature with all the talents of a great actor, suddenly appeared in his twenty-fourth year on the stage at Goodmansfields,[1] and at his first appearance surpassed all the players of his age and became the idol of the people, the spice of society, and the darling of the quality. Almost all the newer English authors, who are so much read, imitated, and aped by us, were his friends. He helped to form them, while they in their turn helped to form him. Man was his study, from the cultured and artificial denizens of the salons of St. James, down to the savage creatures in the eating-houses of St. Giles. He attended the same school as Shakespeare, and, like the latter, did not wait for inspiration, but worked hard (for in England all is not left to genius, as in Germany); by this school I mean London, where a man with such a talent for observation can learn as much by experience in a year as in a whole lifetime spent in some little town, where all have the same hopes and fears, the same subjects for wonder and gossip, and nothing is out of the ordinary. I am therefore not surprised that now and then a man is developed there whose works may hereafter be used by persons from other places, with more limited experience, as a measure of their growth in the knowledge of human nature; that is to say, the more a man has within himself, the more he will gain from reading them. I am, however, surprised that London does not produce more such men; not, indeed, more Garricks, Hogarths, or Fieldings, but persons in some different line, while of like capacities. Knowledge of the world makes an author excel in whatever he attempts. It lends, if not in every case to his matter, yet always to his manner, a vigour

---

[1] Garrick's first appearance on the stage was on 19 October 1741 in *Richard III*. The playbill runs: 'The Part of King Richard by a Gentleman (who never appeared on any stage).'

with which no imitations by some marvellous provincial wit can compete, however differently he himself, his coterie, or his little town may think, as it needs must under the circumstances. Therefore a man with some knowledge of the world may easily see that on the stage Garrick makes use of lore which one would almost pronounce wasted on such surroundings, but probably only as long as one had as yet none to waste oneself. It may well be that, when I was looking at Garrick, many pairs of eyes may have gazed at him, seeing more in him than I could perceive, and yet not finding all that they sought. If Garrick were representing, for example, a great glutton, and wanted to feel with his fingers to see whether his capon or pheasant on the spit was done to a turn, I dare swear that he would probe it with the fourth finger of his left hand. In all the others there would be too much strength and too little feeling. But a man must discover such things for himself; in attempting to describe them for others, he risks being laughed at just when he fancies himself most wise.

Beyond those qualities essential to a good actor, this man possesses several others, which would make a man's fortune in any rank of life and could take him as far as he wished to go. Among them I count his gift for perceiving very quickly the weaknesses both of individuals and the general public. This enables him in case of need to enhance natural beauties by side-play, without which they could never have made the same impression in some particular year, or, one might almost say, on some special day. I have myself remarked that when, on the occasion of some new venture, there is an absence either of loud applause or of the usual death-like silence of the audience, he is sure to evoke them by some happy turn before the end of the representation.

Now, my dear B., in case you should picture from what I have said a Garrick other than he is, you shall now see him through my eyes in a few scenes. Being so disposed, I will to-day take those from *Hamlet*, where the ghost appears to him. You know him already in these scenes from Master Partridge's excellent description in *The Foundling*. Mine shall not supersede this, but only explain it.

Hamlet appears in a black dress, the only one in the whole court, alas! still worn for his poor father, who has been dead scarce a couple of months. Horatio and Marcellus, in uniform, are with him, and they are awaiting the ghost; Hamlet has folded his arms under his cloak and pulled his hat down over his eyes; it is a cold night and just twelve o'clock; the theatre is darkened, and the whole audience of some thousands are as quiet, and their faces as motionless, as though they were painted on the walls of the theatre; even from the farthest end of the playhouse one could hear a pin drop. Suddenly, as Hamlet moves towards the back of the stage slightly to the left and turns his back on the audience, Horatio starts, and saying: 'Look, my lord, it comes,' points to the right, where the ghost has already appeared and stands motionless, before any one is aware of him. At these words Garrick turns sharply and at the same moment staggers back two or three paces with his knees giving way under him; his hat falls to the ground and both his arms, especially the left, are stretched out nearly to their full length, with the hands as high as his head, the right arm more bent and the hand lower, and the fingers apart; his mouth is open: thus he stands rooted to the spot, with legs apart, but no loss of dignity, supported by his friends, who are better acquainted with the apparition and fear lest he should collapse. His whole demeanour is so expressive of terror that it made my flesh creep even before he began to speak. The almost terror-struck silence of the audience, which preceded this appearance and filled one with a sense of insecurity, probably did much to enhance this effect. At last he speaks, not at the beginning, but at the end of a breath, with a trembling voice: 'Angels and ministers of grace defend us!' words which supply anything this scene may lack and make it one of the greatest and most terrible which will ever be played on any stage. The ghost beckons to him; I wish you could see him, with eyes fixed on the ghost, though he is speaking to his companions, freeing himself from their restraining hands, as they warn him not to follow and hold him back. But at length, when they have tried his patience too far, he turns his face towards them, tears himself with great violence from their grasp, and draws his sword on them with a swiftness that makes one shudder, saying: 'By Heaven! I'll make a ghost of him that lets me.' That is enough for them. Then he stands with his sword upon guard against the spectre, saying: 'Go on, I'll follow thee,' and the ghost goes off the stage. Hamlet still remains motionless, his sword held out so as to make him keep his distance, and at length, when the spectator can no longer see the ghost, he begins slowly to follow him, now standing still and then going on, with sword still upon guard, eyes fixed on the ghost, hair disordered, and out of breath, until he too is lost to sight. You can well imagine what loud applause accompanies this exit. It begins as soon as the ghost goes off the stage and lasts until Hamlet also disappears. What an amazing triumph it is. One might think that such applause in one of the first playhouses in the world and from an audience of the greatest sensibility would fan into flame every spark of dramatic genius in a spectator. But then one perceives that to act like Garrick and to write like Shakespeare are the effects of very deep-seated causes. They are certainly imitated; not they, but rather their phantom self, created by the imitator according to the measure of his own powers. He often attains to and even surpasses this phantom, and nevertheless falls far short of the true original. The house-painter thinks his work as perfect as, or even more so than that of the artist. Not every player who can always command the applause of a couple of hundred people or so is on that account a Garrick; and not every writer who has learnt the trick of blabbing a few so-called secrets of human nature in archaic prose, outraging language and propriety by his bombast, is on that account a Shakespeare.

The ghost was played by Mr. Bransby.[1] He looked, in truth, very fine, clad from head to foot in armour, for which a suit of steel-blue satin did duty; even his face is hidden, except for his pallid nose and a little to either side of it.

This is enough for to-day concerning Mr. Garrick, but I cannot possibly end without again considering the actors of my native land. Some of my friends in Germany feared lest I should become so spoilt by my frequent visits to the English playhouses that I should henceforth have no taste for those in Germany. Thank Heaven! my little bit of travelling has not yet taught me false pride; and it would in truth be this or something even worse, if my present convictions prevented me from recognizing the merits of our own players. On the contrary, I shall henceforth admire the good creatures more than ever, because they have attained to an amazing degree of excellence, considering the conditions that prevail in our country, as I can now perceive better than before. Of those I have seen in Göttingen, Hanover, and Hamburg (I am not acquainted with any other playhouses), not only are many fit to play at Drury Lane, but some would even cause a sensation. With the exception of Mr. Garrick there is on the English stage at present not a single

[1] One of the Drury Lane company. Died March 1789.

player so versatile as Herr Eckhof,[1] for example, although there are several who have attained to a high degree of excellence, if not to perfection, in special parts. At Drury Lane there are, for instance, King,[2] Smith,[3] Dodd,[4] Parsons,[5] Palmer,[6] and, above all, that droll fellow Weston; and at Covent Garden, Barry Lewis (who promises to be an actor of great versatility), Lee,[7] Macklin,[8] Shuter,[9] and Woodward.[10] But even Mr. Smith of Drury Lane, a tolerably popular actor and handsome man, who takes Garrick's parts, Hamlet, Richard III, and so forth, and is moreover much applauded in them, at the beginning of the winter before Garrick appears, and towards the end when he again takes his departure, is far inferior to Herr Eckhof. The reason for this is that he does not get his art from the fountain-head, not having that knowledge of human nature which Herr Eckhof must possess. This becomes evident from the following anecdote, which I have from a reliable source. Several years ago when indeed Mr. Smith was as yet hardly the man he is now, he started with terror when playing Hamlet in the scene described above, but then, taking off his hat, made a low and respectful bow to the shade of his august father. It is in such ways that those persons who fancy that imitation answers the purpose give themselves away unawares. Herr Eckhof neither would nor could have done such a thing, even when only twelve years old. On this account they then dubbed Mr. Smith 'Monsieur Hamlet', though the name is now forgotten.

Some months ago I read in an English newspaper with the deepest emotion of the death of the younger Mamsell Ackermann. Is it not sad, my dear B.? I cannot bring myself to inquire which

[1] Hans Konrad Eckhof, 1720–78. A native of Hamburg, famous actor.
[2] Thomas King, 1730–1805, actor and playwriter. He had a wandering career at fairs and the like and first appeared in London at Drury Lane. He rose rapidly at Smock Alley Theatre. He was the first Sir Peter Teazle.
[3] William Smith, 1730–1819, known as 'Gentleman Smith'. Famous as Charles Surface.
[4] James William Dodd, 1740–96. He played over thirty years at Drury Lane. One of his principal parts was Sir Andrew Aguecheek.
[5] William Parsons, 1736–95, actor and painter. He had a long career at Drury Lane, Haymarket, in over 150 parts.
[6] John Palmer, 1742–98, greatly noted as Joseph Surface. It is recorded that he played over 300 parts.
[7] John Lee, died 1781, actor and adapter of plays.
[8] Charles Macklin, died 1797, actor and stage manager.
[9] Edward Shuter, 1728–76, a celebrated comedian in a wide range of parts.
[10] Henry Woodward, 1714–77, prominent comedian.

English actress she may have equalled: at present it would be too melancholy an affair, and at no time would it be an easy one. There is not one of her own age who is what she was, and she might well have surpassed under similar conditions the two or three older ones who at present surpass her, by her eight and twentieth year. In the meantime she has shown what we can produce in Germany in our little hothouses. Would that our plants might enjoy the sun which they have in England where, moreover, they are safe from the lightning, for which in Germany no Franklin has as yet discovered a conductor, although many a city and township has its Richmann, who had to forfeit his own life for his presumption in playing with it.[1] I am, &c.

II

London, 10 October 1775.

I am writing to you again, my most honoured B., without awaiting an answer to my last letter with questions which would have given me a clue to a quicker way of satisfying your wishes. Just now I have time and a mind to seek for it, while both might be lacking at the moment when you give me the clue. Let us see, therefore, whether I cannot manage without it.

When I have observed Mr. Garrick standing there in full force and vigour, I have sometimes wondered, if I may say so, whether many players, not so excellently formed by nature as he, might compensate for this in some degree by art. I should like to know whether on the stage they pad themselves out, just as they paint, in order to appear more handsome. If they do so, as I can scarce doubt, it is, in truth, clear that this art is not everywhere understood. The bone formation of many German players is not so bad as the covering of muscle and fat, which is perpetually worn away by time and illness, and in the Parisian provinces of our native land, hunger and care also. The audience cannot feel, will not hear, but needs must see, a refreshing certainty and firmness of movement and reserve of vigour; and these may on occasion be seen in a pair of bony shoulders, cylindrical shanks, empty sleeves, or spindle legs. I am convinced that it is often a very slight malformation of

---

[1] Benjamin Franklin, 1706–90, in 1752 by an extremely dangerous experiment proved the identity of lightning and the electric spark. Georg Wilhelm Richmann, 1711–53, Professor at St. Petersburg, lost his life when attempting the same experiment on 6 August the following year.

the arm which makes an actor's gestures (*portebras*) look somewhat clumsy. A pillar whose cube is only one sixth higher than it is broad looks to an expert eye unfit to hold up the building. And what is the beauty of a pillar in comparison with that of the human form, of which the eye is the natural judge, kept alert by a hundred different interests.

Portebras reminds me of Mrs. Yates,[1] the first actress in the high tragic style at Garrick's playhouse. This woman is no longer young, and being, moreover, one of the leaner kind, her arms are probably none too fine. I have never, indeed, seen her arms bare nor even covered only by gloves. Even when playing characters who would have been loath to hide a pretty arm, she wears a full sleeve, which does not, however, appear empty, falling from the shoulder and gradually narrowing until it fits tightly round the hand. In order to avoid the monotony which such a costume might give to her arms, she sometimes winds round them a trimming that forms a marked contrast to the colour of her dress. The pleasing conical shape of the sleeves lends the arm an appearance of vigour, while it does not only dispose, but positively impels, every spectator to imagine the most lovely arm concealed by it. She is so skilled in the management of her arms that from this woman alone could be made an abstract of the art of gesticulation. Players should not neglect any means of producing this illusion of dexterity, when it is denied them by nature; for, although the spectators cannot all say with precision where the fault lies, they feel none the less that it is there, on account of the weakened impression made on them by the representation, and this is especially the case where they have not learnt out of books to prate of these matters.

The indescribably pleasing lightness, vigour, and certainty of movement (these are the best words I can find for them) in which Mr. Garrick excels, were not, I expect, acquired without difficulty, although I will not deny that the excellent proportion of his limbs helped to produce them. I fear that many years and much grilling labour went towards the exercising of his body, before it attained at length to this effortless ease, which, enhanced by perpetual observation of handsome men, admired and envied by persons of both sexes, now looks as though it came to him naturally. Just as the ease and vigour in the style of the writers of antiquity may not

[1] Mrs. Mary Ann Yates, 1728–87, certainly one of the greatest English tragic actresses, acted first in Dublin, then in 1753 at Drury Lane.

have been the fruits of a Land of Cockaigne but rather the outcome of distinct conceptions, gained by much deep study, and the quintessence of whole tomes of exercises, which they burnt.

This man is, moreover, buoyed up by a sense of his own superiority. He has nothing to fear. The whole public looks up to him, and the few who may be greater than he are assuredly such as would keep silence. It is no wonder that their enthusiasm sometimes sheds a light on him, while throwing into the shade all the other players. There is in all he does and says not the slightest trace of that anxious striving to please which makes so many players unpleasing. Further; when he represents a courtier one does not see some poor devil playing a part, but a very man of the world; a man who shines to-night in a tinsel court at Drury Lane, and to-morrow in the golden one at St. James's. How many courtiers—or, shall I say rather, how many Hamlets—are there in the world, who are what this man is within his four walls? So much for a few fresh strokes of the brush towards his portrait as Garrick. Now I will proceed to add a few to Hamlet.

In the excellent soliloquy: 'O that this too, too solid flesh would melt,' &c., he again applies, to make use of astronomical terms, a number of small equations, by which he heightens the actions of an average man, giving them individuality by touches of truth and exactitude. Garrick is completely overcome by tears of grief, felt with only too good cause, for a virtuous father and on account of a light-minded mother, who not only wears no mourning, but feels no sorrow, at a time when all the toadies should still be wearing black; tears which flow all the more unrestrainedly, perhaps, since they are the sole relief of an upright heart in such a conflict of warring duties. The last of the words: 'So excellent a King', is utterly lost; one catches it only from the movement of the mouth, which quivers and shuts tight immediately afterwards, so as to restrain the all too distinct expression of grief on the lips, which could easily tremble with unmanly emotion. This manner of shedding tears, which betrays both the heavy burden of grief on his heart and the manly spirit which suffers under it, is irresistibly poignant. But as soon as one is attuned to Shakespeare's mind, each word, as Garrick speaks it, pierces one's heart. At the end of the soliloquy his grief is mingled with righteous anger, and on one occasion, when he brings his arm down sharply in a single movement, so as to lend emphasis to one word of invective, his voice is choked with emotion, when the audience is not expecting it, and he can only bring out this word after some moments amidst his tears. At this point I and my neighbour, to whom I had not as yet uttered a word, looked at each other and spoke. It was quite irresistible.

The famous soliloquy: 'To be or not to be,' &c., does not naturally make the same impression on the auditor, and cannot, in truth, do so. But it produces an infinitely greater effect than could be expected of an argument on suicide and death in a tragedy; and this is because a large part of the audience not only knows it by heart as well as they do the Lord's Prayer, but listens to it, so to speak, as if it were a Lord's Prayer, not indeed with the profound reflections which accompany our sacred prayer, but with a sense of solemnity and awe, of which some one who does not know England can have no conception. In this island Shakespeare is not only famous, but holy; his moral maxims are heard everywhere; I myself heard them quoted in Parliament on 7 February, a day of importance. In this way his name is entwined with most solemn thoughts; people sing of him and from his works, and thus a large number of English children know him before they have learnt their A.B.C. and creed.

Hamlet, who is in mourning, as I have already reminded you, appears here, having already begun to feign madness, with his thick hair dishevelled and a lock hanging over one shoulder; one of his black stockings has slipped down so as to show his white socks, and a loop of his red garter is hanging down beyond the middle of the calf. Thus he comes on to the stage sunk in contemplation, his chin resting on his right hand, and his right elbow on his left, and gazes solemnly downwards. And then, removing his right hand from his chin, but, if I remember right, still supporting it with his left hand, he speaks the words 'To be or not to be,' &c., softly, though, on account of the absolute silence (not because of some particular talent of the man's, as they say even in some of the newspapers), they are audible everywhere.

Here I must make a short comment on the language. In the fourth line of this soliloquy some suggest the reading 'against assailing troubles', instead of 'against a sea of troubles', because one cannot take arms against the sea.[1] In spite of this Mr. Garrick says 'against a sea of troubles'. I merely quote Garrick's opinion, and do not go into the question of the authorities he follows. It

[1] This reading was suggested in Sir T. Hanmer's edition (Oxford, 1743-4).

would not be easy to do so here, and you can settle the matter in a moment in the Library at Göttingen.

Ophelia's dress, likewise, after she has lost her reason, is disordered, as far as propriety allows. She was played by Mrs. Smith,[1] a young woman and a good singer, who is admirably suited to the part (although she has not enough vivacity for several others that she takes). Her long flaxen hair hung partly down her back, and partly over her shoulders; in her left hand she held a bunch of loose straw, and her whole demeanour in her madness was as gentle as the passion which caused it. The songs, which she sang charmingly, were fraught with such plaintive and tender melancholy that I fancied that I could still hear them far into the night, when I was alone. Shakespeare makes this whole scene so moving as to cause one actual pain and leave a sore place in the heart, which goes on throbbing until one could wish never to have seen poor, unhappy Ophelia. I wish that Voltaire might have been here and heard Mrs. Smith's interpretation of Shakespeare! This remarkable man would, I believe, almost have repented of what he said against these scenes. I am sure that if I had written any such thing—of course with the wit of a Voltaire and his influence on weak minds— and had afterwards seen what I have been seeing, I should, forsooth, have asked the forgiveness of Shakespeare's spirit in the newspapers. Voltaire has, however, gained one victory at Drury Lane. The gravediggers' scene is omitted. They retain it at Covent Garden. Garrick should not have done this. To represent so ancient and superb a piece in all its characteristic rude vigour in these insipid times, when even in this country the language of nature is beginning to yield to fine phrases and conventional twaddle, might have arrested this decline, even if it could not put a stop to it.

I must pass by some of the finest scenes, as, for instance, that in which he instructs the players, and the one where he pierces his mother's heart by his comparison of his uncle and his father, and the ghost appears forthwith; one blow after another, before one has had time to recover from the first. But one could go on for ever, so I will here conclude the tragedy and give you only a short farce.

Sir John Brute is not merely a dissolute fellow, but Garrick makes him an old fop also, this being apparent from his costume. On top of a wig, which is more or less suitable for one of his years,

[1] Mrs. Smith was the sister of Mrs. Bates, who acted at Covent Garden.

he has perched a small, beribboned, modish hat so jauntily that it covers no more of his forehead than was already hidden by his wig. In his hand he holds one of those hooked oaken sticks, with which every young poltroon makes himself look like a devil of a fellow in the Park in the morning (as they call here the hours between 10 and 3). It is in fact a cudgel, showing only faint traces of art and culture, as is generally the case also with the lout who carries it. Sir John makes use of this stick to emphasize his words with bluster, especially when only females are present, or in his passion to rain blows where no one is standing who might take them amiss.

In all playhouses there is generally one or another of the actors who can represent a drunken man very tolerably. The reason for this is not far to seek. There is no lack of opportunity for observation, and, whatever may be the main motive of the play, such a part must, in the nature of things, have no narrow or sharply defined limits. In spite of this Mr. Garrick plays the drunken Sir John in such a way that I should certainly have known him to be a most remarkable man, even if I had never heard anything of him and had seen him in one scene only in this play. At the beginning his wig is quite straight, so that his face is full and round. Then he comes home excessively drunk, and looks like the moon a few days before its last quarter, almost half his face being covered by his wig; the part that is still visible is, indeed, somewhat bloody and shining with perspiration, but has so extremely amiable an air as to compensate for the loss of the other part. His waistcoat is open from top to bottom, his stockings full of wrinkles, with the garters hanging down, and, moreover—which is vastly strange—two kinds of garters; one would hardly be surprised, indeed, if he had picked up odd shoes. In this lamentable condition he enters the room where his wife is, and in answer to her anxious inquiries as to what is the matter with him (and she has good reason for inquiring), he, collecting his wits, answers: 'Wife, as well as a fish in the water'; he does not, however, move away from the doorpost, against which he leans as closely as if he wanted to rub his back. Then he again breaks into coarse talk, and suddenly becomes so wise and merry in his cups that the whole audience bursts into a tumult of applause. I was filled with amazement at the scene where he falls asleep. The way in which, with shut eyes, swimming head, and pallid cheeks, he quarrels with his wife, and, uttering a sound where 'r' and 'l' are blended, now appears to abuse her, and then to enunciate in thick tones moral precepts, to which he himself forms the most horrible contradiction; his manner, also, of moving his lips, so that one cannot tell whether he is chewing, tasting, or speaking: all this, in truth, as far exceeded my expectations as anything I have seen of this man. If you could but hear him articulate the word 'prerogative'; he never reaches the third syllable without two or three attempts. Vanbrugh has made an excellent use of this. It is the perfect watchword, the signal for blows of ale-house politicians in England; they do not trouble themselves about its meaning, but it can set them all by the ears when the protagonists have reached the point of being unable to pronounce it. But however excellently they represent this play, for Lady Brute was played by Miss Young[1] and Lady Fancyful by the famous Mrs. Abington,[2] I am yet convinced that it would be better never to produce it. They have, indeed, altered the shameful scene where Sir John Brute disguises himself as a parson and wrestles with the watch, so that he performs these mighty deeds clad only in a hooped petticoat, *saloppe*, and head-dress, to which there can be no objection; but in spite of this there are here and there abominable things, offending ear and eye.

As I remarked above, Garrick possesses a talent for giving individuality to everything in so high a degree that it contributes not a little to his superiority; and yet one would have thought that this might easily be acquired, at least to a certain extent, from the observation not of actors, but of polite society. If the actors but knew what to observe! A stage puppet will remain frozen and lifeless, in spite of the outfit provided for him by the author, especially when this is all French trash, unless the actor can clothe him afresh in living warmth. Garrick will sooner thrust his left hand into his right-hand pocket, if need arise, than let go a pinch of snuff that he has between the fingers of his right hand. When disguised as a raw, awkward fellow, he can carry his best Spanish cane in such a way that you might think he was taking it for his master to the silversmith's to be sold, or that it contained a barometer. A table of equations containing such features would be no small boon to

---

[1] Miss Elizabeth Young, *c.* 1744–97, wife of Alexander Pope, and a great actress.

[2] Frances Abington, 1737–1815, first appeared at the Haymarket in 1755 in the *Busybody*, played at Bath, and then at Drury Lane, and five years in Ireland, the most noted Beatrice of Shakespeare.

players, and, between ourselves, to dramatic authors and novelists. All of them (one can speak in general terms, for there are but two or three exceptions, whose worth is well known) write as though they lack matter for observation, or wit to make use of it, and most of them, as though they lacked both. If a lawyer is to be represented, you may depend upon it that it will be all *Leges* and Justinian, the advocate appearing all the time with long-winded speeches and lengthy lawsuits; the ensign curses or talks of a thrashing; and your philanthropists go about, as they are to the life, with a tear in their eye and hard cash in their hand. All that is tolerably good, and may do well enough for sixth form boys and for nine out of ten of the καλοῖς κἀγαθοῖς who express their opinions of books in print. But is that Shakespeare's art? As little, forsooth, as making crucifixes is Christianity. I should have thought that the lawyer, the inn-keeper, the merchant, the tradesman, the barber, the shopman, the country-town official, each had his own politics, his own canons of good taste, his own physiognomy and astronomy. Whoever takes pleasure in looking for these things will soon find them. They are most apparent when such persons wish to impress their subordinates by showing themselves on an equal footing with some expert. I was once showing the crescent moon through a very powerful telescope to a company who knew little or nothing of astronomy. Several of them asked whether there were not spots on the glass. The *maculae* on the moon do, indeed, bear some resemblance to raindrops on a window-pane, in which the opposite houses appear dark and the sky light. This was all very well, for they were females, who made no pretention to learning and went by the evidence of their senses. But then a man, waving aside the ignorant creatures, suddenly turned to me and said: 'Pray tell me if these drops are not really what is called *influxum lunae physicum*?' Or again, in a very mixed company in an inn, another asked me: 'Tell me, Sir, is it not the elevation of the pole when one goes out in the evening and looks at the sky.' As he said this, he was in fact gazing upwards at such an angle as suggested to me that some one must have shown him the pole star. An example of a confused idea, expressed in a confused manner. Can you guess who these people were? Lavater's[1] angel, who from a single tooth can reconstruct the man to whom it belonged, would know in a moment. I will tell you, in case you wish to propound the riddle to any one else. The latter was a

[1] See note, p. 102.

wealthy and conceited shopkeeper, who wished to pass himself off
as a man of learning to some of those present, even if he lowered
himself in the estimation of the rest; and the first was a catholic
canon, who was not quite sober. This is enough for to-day. On
some future occasion I will tell you something of Garrick's portraits,
and perhaps something of Weston, and the females, probably also
of Gabrielli,[1] whom, I expect, you know from Brydone's Journey.
She is here, and is shortly to appear as Dido. Farewell.

III

London, 30 November 1775.

It is on account of a disagreeable occurrence, the indisposition
of one of my fellow travellers, that I have quite unexpectedly found
time, my dear B., to keep my promise of writing to you once more
before my departure, which would otherwise have been impossible.
I am, in truth, all the more ready to devote part of this time to such
an occupation, since it both gives me the pleasure I always take in
any intercourse with you, and also compensates for a lack of congenial society, under which I am suffering here in some degree,
after having already taken leave and being declared *pro absente*.

Although I have not in the least forgotten that I promised to
write to you concerning Weston and some actresses on the English
stage, I will begin once more with Garrick.

I believe that I have already told you that he plays Hamlet in
a French suit. That seems, in truth, an odd choice. I have frequently heard him blamed for this, though never between the acts,
nor on the way home, nor at supper after the play; but always after
the impression made by him has had time to fade; and the intellect
has revived sufficiently for cool discussion, in which, as you know,
learned is taken to be synonymous with good, and striking with
ingenious. I must confess that this criticism has never appealed
to me. And pray consider whether it was so very difficult to be
thus cautious.

For my part, I am convinced that Garrick is an extremely ingenious man, who, being able to gauge to a nicety the taste of his
fellow countrymen, certainly attempts nothing on the stage without
good reason, and, besides, has a whole house full of ancient costumes;
he is, moreover, a man who makes use of his experience of everyday

[1] See Letter 21.

life at fitting times and places, not for any monstrous heightening of his eloquence, but for the promotion of a harmonious growth of common sense. Is it likely that such a man could not comprehend what every London Macaroni would dare swear was as plain as a pikestaff? He, who thirty years ago had already become that which one would scarce concede to most of his critics at the present time. So instead of agreeing, I began to reflect as to what can have moved him to do such a thing. I pondered every aspect of the matter, so as to explain it, at least to my own satisfaction, until at last I found myself in agreement with what are presumably Garrick's sentiments, on the second occasion on which I saw *Hamlet* played, at the moment when he draws his sword on Horatio. As far as I am concerned, he is entirely justified; and would, indeed, in my opinion, lose much of his effect if he appeared otherwise. Each one to his taste, *damus petimusque*. I am well aware that in such matters one can be led by hair-splitting and over-refinement into the same error as another will come to far more comfortably and quickly by overhaste. Be that as it may, I cannot pass over in silence my reasons, which, though not perhaps those of Garrick himself, may yet serve to guide a few thoughtful actors to better things.

It seems to me that, if we are not vastly learned, ancient costumes on the stage are too reminiscent of a disguise worn at a masquerade, which is, indeed, pleasing, if it be pretty; but the trifling pleasure it gives can seldom contribute much to the sum total of all which heightens the impression of a play. It has the same effect on me as a German book printed in Latin characters, which in my opinion is a kind of translation. Short as is the time I spend in translating these symbols into my old Darmstadt A B C, it detracts nevertheless from the impression. An epigram would lose the whole of its pristine vigour if one had to spell it out at first sight, for example, with book upside down. It is a sin and a shame without any necessity to sever even one of the delicate threads on which our pleasure depends. I have therefore come to the conclusion that we should by all means retain modern dress in a play, so long as it does not offend the susceptibilities of imperious pedants. Our French coats have long ago been advanced to the dignity of a tunic, and their creases to the importance of play of the features; while all wrestling, writhing, fencing, and falling in an unfamiliar dress we can, indeed, understand, but do not feel sensibly. I am entirely sensible of the fall of a hat in the course of a struggle, but much less so of that of a helmet, which might be ascribed to the awkwardness of the actor and appear ridiculous, since I have no notion how firmly it is possible to fix on a helmet. When Garrick, in the situation mentioned above, had partly turned his back on the audience, and I perceived that his exertions had produced that well-known diagonal crease from the shoulder to the opposite hip, it was, in truth, worth the play of facial expression twice over. In the inky cloak, of which Hamlet once speaks, I should assuredly not have remarked this. A well-formed actor (as all, at any rate, should be who have anything to do with tragedy) will certainly lose something by wearing a costume differing too greatly from such as might have been either earlier or later in life not the least object of any man's desires and the sweetest gratification of youthful vanity; in which, moreover, the eye can detect to a hair's breadth the least excess or deficiency. You must understand, of course, that I do not suggest that Caesar and England's Henries and Richards should appear on the stage in the uniform of the Guards, with scarf and gorget. Every one has acquired at school, and from engravings, medals and firebacks, enough knowledge and antiquarian pride to be sensible of, and resent, these and similar deviations from general custom. I think, however, that where the public is not yet awake to a certain point of antiquarian interest, the player should not be the first to disturb their slumbers. The trifling momentary pleasure, so to speak, given me by the worthless splendour of a masquerade costume, does not make amends for the harm done to the play in every other respect. All the spectators are aware that something is lacking, though all do not believe this to be the cause of it. The taste of an actor of tolerable discernment, who knows the strength and the foibles of the public before which he must appear, in this transcends all rules. In the case I have taken, London, as regards Hamlet the Dane, is in this situation, so is there any need for Garrick to be wise at the expense of both parties? Garrick can well dispense on the one hand with a modicum of praise for his learning, if, on the other, the hearts of thousands are drawn to him.

Now come, my friend, and view this aesthetic shadow play, of which, perhaps, something might have been made by the genius of the Quinquennium, if one of our philosophical Savoyards had been moved to attune his sublime Babel to it; you shall now, even if not given perfect satisfaction, at least be refreshed by variety.

I will conjure up for you in a few scenes the droll Weston, of whom I promised to tell you more when I drew a hasty sketch of his character in my first letter. This odd creature stepped out of the kitchen of St. James, where his father was an under-cook, straight on to the stage; his figure, if one had caught sight of it in the street, would have seemed so little suited to the theatre that it needed, in truth, a Garrick and a Foote to discover its possibilities. This they did. He is a small, wooden-looking man, and therefore his demeanour is most impressive when he stands with hands in his pockets. His features are excessively coarse, the lips somewhat thick, and the nose resembling a shoe-last. But the eyes, which seem scarcely to belong to such a face, betoken the sly rogue who misses nothing, and Garrick's successful rival, in his own line at least. His voice is flat and thick, and he is slow of speech. I have seen such fellows on Sundays in almost all the towns in which I have been, and have no notion whether they were rope-makers or market-gardeners, for they were certainly not sleek and nimble enough to be bakers. I must now enter into details. In the play in which I am now calling him to mind he wore a coat of sky-blue cloth, tinged with mist-colour, a red waistcoat, black breeches, and blue stockings; his buckles were fixed, I thought, excessively far forward on his shoes, and his hair hung loose round his head like bunches of carrots. When he appears on the stage, you would think that some one had made his way in there unnoticed from the street, so natural is his costume, and so unaffected his appearance. This betrays no common talent.

From all this you can see that he will never be as versatile as a chameleon, but he obtains his effects rather by a fox-like astuteness. Nature, which on the one hand seems to have formed him purposely to excite laughter, on the other appears to have deprived him of the faculty of laughing himself. He is always serious, or at best only smiles, and this but seldom; and it is a long time before his whole face is smiling. In one play I saw how a pretty Abigail strokes his cheeks in order to attach him to her lady's interests. His face lit up slowly, indeed, but to such a degree that at least two dozen teeth became visible, of which many were far from small. There was scarce a mouth in the whole playhouse which did not, each in its own way, either laugh or smile with him. He is such a stiff-necked original fellow and so loath to go a step out of his way to adapt himself to a character that the authors have instead adapted the characters to him. They say that Jerry Sneak in Foote's *Mayor of Garratt* which he plays so incomparably is modelled on Weston, which is, indeed, not to be wondered at. The servant in *The Maid of the Oaks*, also, a play of which they make a vast deal of fuss at the moment, is not only played by Weston, but the author has made the servant in this play Weston himself. I mentioned, I believe, in my first letter, a scene in Farquhar's *Stratagem*,[1] in which I saw Garrick and Weston together. I will describe it to you to the best of my ability, although I very much doubt whether my outline will be even tolerable. Both player and spectator are more at home in comedy than in tragedy; and it is easier, I think, to express in words what the player achieves in tragedy by means of the most consummate art, than that which the inexhaustible resources of nature both effect and perceive in comedy. It is impossible to describe a scene such as this, in which the two favourites of an enlightened people strive to add to a fame established long ago; yet without over-acting, since they are kept in check by a most practised judgement. I can do no more than give some hints at random to enable the imagination of others, the scope of which is unknown to me, to conjure up a similar vision.

Garrick plays Archer, a gentleman of quality disguised as a servant for reasons which may easily be guessed; and poor Weston takes the part of Scrub, a tapster in a wretched inn at which the former is lodging, and where all the wants of the stomach and the delights of the palate could be had yesterday, will be there on the morrow, but never to-day. Garrick wears a sky-blue livery, richly trimmed with sparkling silver, a dazzling beribboned hat with a red feather, displays a pair of calves gleaming with white silk, and a pair of quite incomparable buckles, and is, indeed, a charming fellow. And Weston, poor devil, oppressed by the burden of greasy tasks, which call him in ten different directions at once, forms an absolute contrast, in a miserable wig spoilt by the rain, a grey jacket, which had been cut perhaps thirty years ago to fit a better-filled paunch, red woollen stockings, and a green apron. He is all pious astonishment when this gentleman's gentleman[2] (as

---

[1] George Farquhar, 1678–1707, a relative of Londonderry, educated at Trinity College, Dublin. He began life as an actor in Dublin. He ceased acting and took to writing. His first play, *Love and a Bottle*, was given at Drury Lane. His greatest success was *The Beaux' Stratagem* in 1707.

[2] In the original: 'dieser Herr Bediente', cp. Letter 9, p. 67, where the girl who gave the servant this title is, however, described as: 'das Mädchen zu

the Göttingen girl said) appears. Garrick, sprightly, roguish, and handsome as an angel, his pretty little hat perched at a rakish angle over his bright face, walks on with firm and vigorous step, gaily and agreeably conscious of his fine calves and new suit, feeling himself head and shoulders taller beside the miserable Scrub. And Scrub, at the best of times a poor creature, seems to lose even such powers as he had and quakes in his shoes, being deeply sensible of the marked contrast between the tapster and the valet; with dropped jaw and eyes fixed in a kind of adoration, he follows all of Garrick's movements. Archer, who wishes to make use of Scrub for his own purposes, soon becomes gracious, and they sit down together. An engraving has been made of this part of the scene, and Sayer has included a copy of it among his well-known little pictures. But it is not particularly like either Weston or Garrick, and of the latter, in especial, it is an abominable caricature, although there are in the same collection of pictures such excellent likenesses of him as Abel Drugger and Sir John Brute that they can scarce be surpassed. This scene should be witnessed by any one who wishes to observe the irresistible power of contrast on the stage, when it is brought about by a perfect collaboration on the part of author and player, so that the whole fabric, whose beauty depends entirely on correct balance, be not upset, as usually happens. Garrick throws himself into a chair with his usual ease of demeanour, places his right arm on the back of Weston's chair, and leans towards him for a confidential talk; his magnificent livery is thrown back, and coat and man form one line of perfect beauty. Weston sits, as is fitting, in the middle of his chair, though rather far forward and with a hand on either knee, as motionless as a statue, with his roguish eyes fixed on Garrick. If his face expresses anything, it is an assumption of dignity, at odds with a paralysing sense of the terrible contrast. And here I observed something about Weston which had an excellent effect. While Garrick sits there at his ease with an agreeable carelessness of demeanour, Weston attempts, with back stiff as a poker, to draw himself up to the other's height, partly for the sake of decorum, and partly in order to steal a glance now and then, when Garrick is looking the other way, so as to improve on his imitation of the latter's manner. When Archer at last with an easy gesture crosses his legs, Scrub tries to do the same, in which he

Kerschlingröder Feld'. It has not been possible to discover her identity, nor that of the Göttingen girl.

eventually succeeds, though not without some help from his hands, and with eyes all the time either gaping or making furtive comparisons. And when Archer begins to stroke his magnificent silken calves, Weston tries to do the same with his miserable red woollen ones, but, thinking better of it, slowly pulls his green apron over them with an abjectness of demeanour, arousing pity in every breast. In this scene Weston almost excels Garrick by means of the foolish expression natural to him, and the simple demeanour that is apparent in all he says and does and which gains not a little from the habitual thickness of his tones. And this is, indeed, saying a great deal. He has both gods and devils[1] on his side. As the servant in *The Maid of the Oaks* he is in more prosperous circumstances, and finely dressed, but in such a way as to make it obvious not only that this is a rare occurrence, but that he is very ill at ease. His hair had been bundled wretchedly into a *crapaud* which stuck out, and powdered here and there on top and at the sides, only, so it seemed to me, with the fingers or scraps of paper; he wore a grey coat and again red stockings, and had a splendid buttonhole. In this play he is chiefly remarkable for an awkward activity and a kind of unnecessary zeal, which, in spite of the drops of perspiration wrung from him, does much to impede the progress of any matter that he intends to further. He is all eagerness to help, and yet defeats his own ends, but nevertheless clearly thinks himself the hero of the moment, whenever his master is not present. It is owing to him, Mrs. Abington,[2] Mr. Dodd,[3] and the amazing splendour of the decorations, which are reminiscent of the Elysian style of the opera, that this play was represented twenty-three times at the beginning of this year. I should like to describe to you how this man, as the cobbler in the *Devil upon two Sticks*, having taken a pair of shoes from under his coat, puts them into the corner, so as to be able, with a more pleasing deportment, to get on to the footstool which he must mount before Foote makes him a 'Doctor'. But when I peruse hastily what I have said, any inclination to say more of him leaves me. It is, indeed, a pleasure to reduce to its constituent parts the general impression made on one by the sight of such a prodigy, and to set down one's reflections (I have written a vast deal of such descriptions for my own pleasure); but a deliberate attempt to give

[1] In the English playhouses the spectators in the upper gallery are called 'the gods', so the writer had the fancy to call those in the pit and boxes 'the devils'. Author's note.   [2] See p. 19.   [3] Dodd, James William. See note, p. 12.

another a similar pleasure is generally a failure, since the inevitable incompleteness in the number of these fully developed sensations will give the reader ample opportunity, after they have been reduced to clarity, to disregard the ultimate design of the author; or, still worse, to reproach him for having read too much into his subject. I must relate to you two anecdotes of the man which gave me a deeper insight into his mind.

Some years ago this awkward fellow chose on his benefit night to represent—you will never guess what—Richard the Third. That the house would be full to overflowing Weston probably knew beforehand as surely as you will believe my words. And this is probably the only occasion on which Shakespeare has deliberately been profaned in the playhouse at Drury Lane; though Shuter has often done so at Covent Garden. When I heard of this, I was reminded of the Apes' Laokoon, where the serpent is coiled about the three apes, father and sons, who all three of them shriek most piteously. It must have been vastly absurd. When he died at the end, the spectators insisted that he should rise again and die once more; I dare swear they made enough din to awake any dead man. He should have said in the well-known monologue: 'An ass, an ass, a kingdom for an ass!' The other incident, of which I myself was a witness, redounds more to his credit. In *The Rival Candidates*,[1] that play in which he is coaxed and petted by the girl, this year he spoke the epilogue in the company of a big dog, nearly as high as his waist, which he led by the ring in its collar. It is a most engaging beast and stares up into its droll companion's face, while he is speaking, with an almost human expression; the latter strokes him with so much condescension that it is obvious to all that they are kindred spirits. On the second occasion on which I saw the play Weston, for the first time, wearied of speaking this epilogue and refused to appear; the audience took this in very bad part, and 'Epilogue! Epilogue!' resounded from all the throats which had done their best to wake Richard the Third from the dead; but still Weston did not appear. Several persons left the boxes, but I had made up my mind to await the outcome of the matter. Suddenly there came a shower, first of pears, then oranges, and next quart-bottles, on to the stage, one of them, containing, I should think, three quarts, striking one of the glass chandeliers; and it looked like turning into a riot, when Weston came on the stage with

[1] *The Rival Candidates*, by Henry Bate (Sir Henry Bate Dudley), 1775.

Dragon (that is the dog's name) as calmly as though he were always called for like this. There was a little hissing here and there, but this soon died down. Now there is a passage in the epilogue, in which, I believe, he is speaking of the critics, where he addresses the dog thus: 'But why do you put your tail between your legs, Dragon, they will not hurt you?' On the spur of the moment, without detriment either to rhyme or couplet, Weston altered the passage into: 'And why do you put your tail between your legs, you tom-fool? They won't throw any bottles at your head.' The situation was saved at a very critical juncture by this excessively witty alteration, so aptly expressed in rhyme. There was no end to the clapping and shouting. But Weston did not move a muscle, his face being as expressionless as a brick, not the least trace of pleasure or complacency, no more than on the face of his four-footed friend. But enough for the moment of Weston, concerning whom I am, however, loath to be silent, since it seems to me as though I have not done him justice, because I am not satisfied myself.

Before I come to the females, I will answer yet another question you put in your letter: as to whether Garrick's playing is always wholly faultless, or whether there is ever anything I should have wished otherwise? I will not make so bold as to point out any faults of Garrick's to you, my dear B.; but, if you wish me to describe my own sensations, without any reference to fundamental laws of aesthetics, and to tell you what I have sometimes found unpleasing, I shall be more willing to comply, although my views can have little importance. Now you must bear in mind that he now only stages plays which he has made entirely his own, and in which he and his picked company have benefited by the criticism of the greatest connoisseurs of human nature for more than a quarter of a century. One can fancy that he first let his stocking hang down on the advice of a Fielding, and perched his hat so charmingly at an angle on that of a Sterne or a Goldsmith. Under these circumstances, my friend, there is much to be learnt, and little with which to find fault. Further, I cannot deny that one is dazzled, to a greater or lesser degree, by his fame; it is, in truth, no small pleasure, I might almost say good fortune, to sit, before the curtain is raised, in front of a stage on which a man will in a few minutes appear whom all will acclaim as the first player of modern times: who is, besides, the friend, master, and pupil of some of the greatest writers of this century. Does that go for nothing? In order to see Garrick play I once set out at half past nine in the morning on a journey of six German miles, missed my dinner, and did not eat until after eleven o'clock in the evening. I was sensible at once of delighted expectation and of anxiety when I heard the music begin that was played before the representation in which I saw him for the first time. Is this at all surprising? If Garrick had spoken with the same power and moved hearts so deeply under warmer skies from a narrower and higher stage, even his rags would have produced a similar effect. Such is human nature, and will be so until the end of the world. I can remember only one occasion when Garrick, who was playing Hamlet, said something in a manner which made a bad impression on me and was not attuned to my mood, which may, indeed, itself have been out of harmony. I will tell you what it was. Before the beginning of the monologue, following the scene in which the ghost discloses the murder to Hamlet, Garrick appears so deeply affected that he stands, as Hamlet himself would have done, rooted to the spot and like one distraught. When at last the stupefaction into which the excellent prince has been plunged by open tombs, unparalleled horrors, and a father's blood crying to Heaven, gradually gives way, and his gloomy and painful sensations find vent in coherent words and crystallize in his secret resolve, Shakespeare has so contrived that Hamlet's reflections and words bear witness to the deep and tumultuous feelings of which they are born; Garrick for his part also, as you can well imagine, contrives that every gesture would make even a deaf spectator aware of the gravity and importance of the words which they accompany. But in my opinion an exception must be made of one line, which, as Garrick spoke it then, would certainly have pleased neither a deaf, nor a blind, spectator. He uttered the physiognomical observations, which he also notes down on his tablets: that one may smile and smile, and be a villain, with an expression and a tone of petty mockery, almost as if he wished to describe a man who smiled perpetually and yet was a villain. I cannot deny that, in the frame of mind I was in at the moment, it struck me so forcibly as to rouse me entirely.

Alas for my letter about Garrick, if you and your friends are not in agreement with my sentiments. But I have no fear of this; for at the second representation of *Hamlet* which I attended, I was gratified and charmed to hear him declaim the same words in a manner entirely in accord with my own sentiments, namely, in the purposeful tone of one bent on immediate action. The smile of the villain to whom Hamlet was referring was fraught on the one hand with too grave import, and on the other with too much horror, to be spoken of in a monologue in cold-blooded mimicry and ridicule. The lips which have smiled thus must be taught gravity by death at Hamlet's hands (and in no other manner), and the sooner the better. What moved Garrick to speak them as he did on the former occasion I cannot conceive. I thought that perhaps it may not be easy to utter the sweet and gentle words, 'smile and smile', without some expression at least reminiscent of a smile; but now I believe it to be rather a deliberate experiment than an involuntary trick of his tongue and the adjacent organs. Is not this, in truth, amazing? I only became aware of it when I attempted to defend the man's art at the expense of his understanding. So, not a word more of the matter.

Of all the actresses here, Mrs. Barry[1] is, in my opinion, the greatest, or at least the most versatile, being in this respect the only one who could bear comparison with Garrick. She can be trimly laced up like a saucy little waiting maid, and trip about so coyly and with such charming self-complacency that all the young misses and all the tall servants in the whole house lose their hearts to her; or, on the other hand, she can sweep in with a cascade of rustling and rippling silk behind her, with an upright carriage and head turned, as though her vanity impelled her to feast her eyes on the set of her train. She is a great beauty, being even by the light of day and without paint, so they tell me, remarkably handsome, and moreover, a born actress. Her native place is lovely, romantic Bath, where her father was an apothecary. In her tenth year (as I have been told by a lady who was acquainted with her at that time), she would cast aside her knitting, creep up to the garret with her Shakespeare, and declaim to the chimneys. Her beauty has something saint-like about it, and the prevailing impression made by her demeanour and the sound of her excessively charming voice is one of gentle innocence and an obliging amiability. A woman perfect in the sight of God and man! Gentle, yielding, and of a temper as little satirical as heroic. She will start at the sound of a

[1] Mrs. Ann Barry, 1734–1801, the wife of Spranger Barry, 1719–77, acted in Dublin, mainly in tragedy; played first in London in 1767, obtained a reputation as Cordelia; was best in comedy.

'God damn!' as though a bomb had exploded. I saw her as Cordelia in *King Lear*, when, raising her large eyes, gleaming with tears, to heaven and silently wringing her hands, she hastens towards her forlorn old father and embraces him with great propriety of demeanour and, so it seemed to me, the radiant countenance of one transfigured. In this remarkable scene she surpasses all other actresses in the same style, and it still provides a feast for my imagination and will live in my memory until my dying day. When I was here five years ago, I saw her as Desdemona in *Othello*. I must certainly have told you of this in Göttingen. I can scarce remember ever having felt so strong a bias with regard to a play as on that occasion. I still think that Reddish,[1] who played the devilish Iago, an odious creature. Alas for all lips and noses which resemble his, if ever I write a treatise on physiognomy!

At that time Mrs. Barry was still at Drury Lane, whereas she is now playing at Covent Garden. Mr. Barry, her husband, an actor who was formerly idolized and is still a favourite, has now become old and stiff. Mr. Garrick got rid, therefore, of this excellent woman, probably on account of her husband, who had to be given a large salary and yet was no longer particularly useful, taking in their stead Mr. and Mrs. Yates[2] from Covent Garden. The former is a tolerable comic actor and does not, I fancy, demand much money, while she is, after Mrs. Barry, certainly the first actress in the high tragic style that England possesses. I was informed by a man, who knew it to be a fact, that Mrs. Barry receives £1,800 a year; if I assume that her husband is paid only half this sum, and put the takings, moreover, on their benefit night at £500 (Miss Catley, a roguish singer, who is a great favourite, received on her benefit night £309, to my certain knowledge), this couple enjoys a yearly income of almost 20,000 thalers, although playing only for a few evenings in the winter. It is a fine thing, in truth, to be an actor, if, as is the case with these persons, natural instinct impels one to be a player, even when there is no hope of such remuneration. They spend the summer in a magnificent country seat in Surrey, of which I once had a distant prospect. I remained standing for half an hour, and even then was not weary of contemplating

[1] Samuel Reddish, 1735–85, acted in Richmond and in Dublin, acted first in London 1767 at Drury Lane, and at Covent Garden in 1778 as Hamlet; died insane in 1785.

[2] Richard Yates, 1716–96, a comedian of note. For Mrs. Yates, cf. note, p. 14.

the variety and glamour cast by my fancy over the house and the surrounding country.

Now I come to an actress whom I have already had occasion to mention, Mrs. Abington, a woman so remarkable in more than one respect that I could easily write you a small book about her. And, if I could have succeeded in giving you an exact description of her talents in such a treatise, I should have been prouder of this than of any accepted work in this category. I have neither the time nor the patience even to attempt such a thing in a letter; and assuredly neither adequate knowledge nor experience to achieve it in a fitting manner, judging by the opinion of all the people whom I have heard extolling her. The little I intend to say of her I set down here, because, if I am to fulfil my promise of writing you letters giving you a short account of all the good actresses in London, it would be just as unpardonable to make my excuses and be entirely silent concerning her as to embark on the work I mentioned, to which, in truth, I should not be equal.

Mrs. Abington is as different from Mrs. Yates and Mrs. Barry as the comic from the tragic muse. She is inferior to them, and especially to the latter, in majesty of demeanour and the expression of tender emotion; but she surpasses them in a talent for convincing the innermost heart of the spectators that she does not feel herself to be acting a part, but presenting reality in all its bitter truth, each trifling characteristic feature bearing witness to her own powers of observation. She is superior to them also in her art, which, alas, she practised all too early; and, moreover, in showing off her magnificent form with an agreeable suggestion of doing so intentionally, which marks out this great actress as a pupil in that dangerous school where her charms were matured . . . and met with their reward, even before she went on the stage. She certainly far surpasses all the other English actresses in wit. One perceives that the cardboard world of Drury Lane is too restricted for her, and at the moment at which I am writing it is already more than a surmise that she will at some future time play her part in the greater sphere it reflects. Her face is far from beautiful; she is pale, and yet too proud to paint, her nose is somewhat turned up, and her mouth not finely cut. But from beneath charming eyebrows she casts glances so piercing that they strike terror into those on whom they alight, and are often accompanied by a certain indescribable smile at some piece of folly she has observed. The style of her clothes and head-dress is always in the most exquisite taste, as I have been assured by ladies, whose opinion I adduce both to complement and accredit my own; thus she seldom appears on the stage, when the mode in genteel society does not follow her lead. In silent parts, or when she had said something she wished to emphasize by walking up and down without speaking, she would often, contrary to the habit of players, turn her back on the audience and walk towards the back of the stage. I wish you might have seen the propriety with which she swayed her hips, with each step evincing a mischievous desire to aggravate the glances of imitative envy and admiration with which a thousand pairs of eyes followed her. Little as she is suited to tragedy, she is less so to low comedy. Her speech is slow, and if she wishes to parody absurdities, they must be only such as can be tolerated by propriety and expressed with grace, either affected or unaffected. Thus, while the wife of Harlequin strikes out right and left against the absurdities of the rabble, rich and poor alike, she, according to the accepted rules of proper duelling, attacks the follies of the great. It is here that her main strength lies, and it betrays no little greatness of soul that she disdains all base means of gaining the applause of the crowd. She has a gift for cleansing vulgar parts of the dust of the work-shop and spinning-room; even though one cannot always approve of this, she is so great an artist that the critics are seldom unmerciful or cold-blooded enough to fall foul of something that is in itself, in truth, excellent, because it is out of keeping with the play as a whole. I have often seen her act, sometimes with Garrick. She pleased me best in *The Provoked Wife*; *The Beaux' Stratagem*; *Rule a Wife and have a Wife*; *The Bon Ton*; *Much Ado about Nothing*, and *The Maid of the Oaks*, a play based on a true story and written by General Burgoyne[1] in honour of his niece, Lady Derby. Few plays in the world have been represented with such tasteful splendour and with such complete excellence as this one, for it is highly probable that the author himself picked the actors and drew the characters with their special peculi-

---

[1] Famous for his defeat at Saratoga (17 October 1778) in the War of American Independence. Burgoyne's *Maid of the Oaks* was described in his lifetime as 'a slight performance'. It was occasioned by the *Fête champêtre* given at the Oaks, near Epsom, on the marriage, June 1774, of the Earl of Derby and Lady Betty Hamilton. See *Biographia Dramatica*. Burgoyne married in romantic circumstances Lady Charlotte Stanley, a daughter of the eleventh earl of Derby, so that Lichtenberg is incorrect: the twelfth earl of Derby was his wife's nephew.

arities in view. The scenery was painted by Lutherberg[1] at a cost of about 10,000 thalers.

They say that, chiefly by her wit, she has captivated a man whose wealth, rank, and reputation can be equalled by few in England, and who is by no means a tyro. He is a widower, and made offer to her of a union in which nothing was lacking but the Church's blessing. Since she is only too well acquainted with this kind of union (for Mr. Abington, of whose name and property she has assumed possession, was not legally her husband), she entered into the contract, as they say, under the following conditions: she must be able to receive visits, now as before, from whomsoever she wishes; the Lord must never wait upon her in her house; he must settle on her £50 a week, besides horses and carriage; and, lastly, he must never require her to leave the stage. All this was agreed on. A victory which makes her the envy not only of all those of her own trade, but also of a large number of the more discreet of England's charmers, and is all the more remarkable, since it is founded neither on youth nor a dazzling complexion, nor on any particular beauty of feature. This anecdote, although I cannot vouch for the truth of every detail, does not appear to me to come amiss here, since it serves to bear out much that I have said of this actress. If you wish to see her perfect reflection, buy a certain portrait of her, an excellent mezzotint after the style of that of Reynolds of Elizabeth Judkins. It is, in truth, a model of easy pose, with the hands in a natural attitude, which is probably thanks to the witchery of this charmer herself. It might be studied with profit by many German portrait painters, who appear to borrow their favourite pose for the hands from the position of the wings of a roast fowl. I possess it, and it will probably remain in my small collection of portraits, which, as you know, come and go, like the vile mortals they portray, though in even more fleeting succession. But here I must break off, according to my promise, but I shall again mention this remarkable lady in a part of my letter where you will least look for it.

At Covent Garden Mrs. Hartley[2] also is remarkable. Her great reputation is founded less on her art than on her exquisite form,

[1] De Loutherbourg, Philip James, R.A., 1740–1812. He came from Fulda, and was a son of the court painter at Darmstadt. He came to England in 1771, and made a distinguished position as a scenery designer. He exhibited more than 150 pictures at the Royal Academy.

[2] Elizabeth Hartley, 1751–1824, played mainly in tragedy, attaining to a high degree of excellence; she retired in 1780.

which verges on ideal beauty. The London macaronis have nick-named her the 'Venus dei Medici'. This is not very apt, it seems to me; she is nothing more nor less than a pretty, dainty little pocket Venus; but, if she is a daughter of Jupiter, Juno is assuredly her mother. In Mason's *Elfrida*[1] she takes a part in which she has to kneel down, and all London congregates to see Mrs. Hartley kneel. I saw her once, not, however, on her knees, but as Lady Macbeth. The scene where she comes in walking in her sleep, in a thin white garment, washing the King's blood, of which she is dreaming, from her hands, still hovers before me, although she did not represent it as if she entered into Shakespeare's spirit, which one with voice and demeanour so infinitely amiable, indeed, scarce could do. I felt as if I were watching a saint who had imposed on herself the heavy penance of counterfeiting for a few minutes the gestures of a devil.

Now, my friend, for a change, let us desert for a while the world in a nutshell, Drury Lane and Covent Garden, and descend (for it is a descent, is it not?) to that tinsel nutshell of a world, the Italian Opera at Haymarket. I have seen and heard the adorable Gabrielli[2] and could have conversed with her, had I wished to do so; an introduction was offered me on one or two occasions, and it was, indeed, taken amiss that I refused it. You know her, I am sure, from Brydone's Journeys,[3] in which I had already heard of her in Göttingen. After that description I had an almost greater desire to hear her than Garrick. She had been residing, like myself, for a long time in London before she appeared. That made matters infinitely worse, as you know. Suddenly they announced:

'Opera Dido'
'Dido, Signora Gabrielli.'

I went to the opera an hour in advance, and was refused admittance: the Signora was ill. Some days later it was again announced:

'Dido, Signora Gabrielli.'

I was carried thither in a sedan chair and again refused admittance:

[1] William Mason, 1724–97, poet and scholar, minister and dramatist. *Elfrida* was first produced in 1752.
[2] Catherine Gabrielli, born in Rome in 1730, died 1796, the famous prima donna.
[3] Patrick Brydone, 1736–1818, F.R.S., travelled extensively, experimented in electricity, comptroller of the Stamp Office. He gives an account of Gabrielli in his *Tour through Sicily and Malta*, ii, 232.

the Signora had 'influenza', as in those Italian days in London they called a cold in the head. For the third time I drove there. I had been dining at Dr. Forster's,[1] and, for Gabrielli's sake, had deserted an excessively agreeable company of men of learning, who talked, indeed, of Otaheite and New Zealand as we should of Eimbeck. Again I was sent away: Dido was not yet recovered. At last, a week later, on 11 December of this year, it seemed as though matters were getting serious. The Signora had recovered from the influenza, but London had been seized with a frenzy to see the Signora, worse than any influenza. On this occasion I again went there on foot, two full hours before it began. They took my money, and I ran up the stairs full of pleasure to think that I should at last be able to write to you about Gabrielli, whom I had as yet not seen myself. When I reached the door of the gallery, for which privilege one has to pay three and a half gulden, I saw, by the dim light of a lantern, a lady standing, who had taken care to flatten herself in the angle of the door. She was well wrapped up in a cloak with the hood pulled up, and her face was buried in a feather muff, so that nothing of it was to be seen but part of the forehead and the eyes; this, however, was more than enough to enable me immediately to recognize Mrs. Abington. So of all the 800,000 souls that London contains, Mrs. Abington and I, even if we had not felt the greatest curiosity of all to see Signora Gabrielli, had at least been foremost in paying three and a half gulden to satisfy it. As quickly as I could, I produced my best English, and said: 'I dare swear that it will be very full to-night.' 'Indeed it will,' said she. At that moment our prophecy was fulfilled with a vengeance, and I thought it would be advisable to place myself at the other angle of the tolerably wide door, so that, when the flood-gates were opened, I might at least enjoy the sorry protection of its support against the surge of the on-coming torrent which was to be anticipated; thus our conversation, which had begun so auspiciously, had it not? was interrupted, and I have never had the honour of resuming it. For in the terrific cataract, of which Mrs. Abington and I were the first drops, that burst out as soon as the door was opened, I lost sight of her. But after I had sat down and got my breath again, I discovered that only two persons—presumably husband and wife—were between her and me, and that I was the only one of the five on my side of her

[1] Probably either Johann Georg Adam Forster, 1754–94, the naturalist and traveller, or his father, Johann Reinhold Forster. See Letter of 16 October 1775.

who had the text of the opera. Since Mrs. Abington was always wishing to know when Gabrielli would appear again, my book was passed along to her. When Dido went off the stage for the last time, she handed back my book, and, moreover, for the sake of our former acquaintance at the door, with a curtsey, for which Lord ——, who would have been better able to interpret it than I was, might perhaps have doubled her weekly allowance. What amazing acquaintances one makes on one's travels!

Now quickly, Gabrielli. The curtain went up to the thunder of twenty drums and trumpets, which took away my breath, and Dido Gabrielli, in gold and white silk, rushed along at the head of a silver-clad Carthaginian guard, amidst the applause of all London. To see and hear such a thing is no trifle. Just fancy, among the Carthaginians, quite in the background, I descried our old friend, George H——, in the uniform, scarf, and gorget of the English Guards. He was on guard near the Opera House that evening, and was acquainted with Dido, I suppose. On this occasion he did not chew his pigtail, as he used to in the Weender Strasse, and, with the help of the music, cut a tolerable figure. But this appearance was to me almost the best of the evening. You must imagine Gabrielli as a round-faced creature, short rather than tall, her eyes betraying that she had arrived at the meridian of life; she has not the least command of gesture, and, trusting to her voice, and with three-quarters of her face turned towards the spectators, she warbles her arias in throaty tones, often with strange writhings of the neck, and eyes fixed on some particular point; and there you have her complete. She sang some of the arias excellently, as, for instance, that in the first act:

'Son Regina: e sono amante
E l'imperio io sola voglio,
Del mio Soglio, e del mio cor.
Darmi legge in van pretende
Chi l'arbitrio a me contende
Della gloria, e dell' amor.'

All the same, I think I have heard it better sung in my dreams. In short, I would as soon give up a quarter of an hour on a really good evening at Drury Lane for the sake of this Dido, as a warm and comfortable country house in Buckinghamshire or in the hilly district between Darmstadt and Heidelberg for her pasteboard Carthage. You must not, however, trust entirely to my opinion, although it is in agreement with that of nearly all London; for I am not entirely impartial. To a head like mine, equipped with a pair of untrained, or perhaps rather unspoiled, ears, the delicate titillations of complicated harmony can scarce do much to relieve the acute discomfort caused at every moment by the excessive absurdity of Italian opera. Instead of Virgil's Aeneas, and gallant Montezuma, who had two hundred wives pregnant at the same time, I see here a fat eunuch with calves right down to his heels, putting his hand on his sluggish heart and warbling of love, till a stone would have compassion on him. I neither can nor will say any more. Are you satisfied? But before I leave the subject of the opera, I must tell you something of a young person who is well worth attention, and has, indeed, probably already attracted it. She is a dancer, the fair rival of our adorable Heinel, whom I saw dance at the opera.

Bacelli[1] is a young (or so, at least, she seemed to me), and yet great, mistress in the art of dancing, and a most charming creature. If Bacelli suggests to an Italian ear the word for a kiss, I should think that she called herself Bacelli on the same principle as the Maltese imitator of the nightingale, Rossignol. She is not one of those lean skeletons, painted over with flesh colour, who, when they dance in the moonlight in their ordinary costume, must look like a concourse of spectres in a churchyard. She is plump rather than thin, and has that agreeable length of limb which, even in pretty little creatures, is not necessarily incompatible with majesty of demeanour. Even in her springing movements she retains an indescribable grace: and in more gentle dances the eye scarce knows whether to fix its attention on the arms, the feet, or some other feature of her swaying form. It is most charming to watch how, at the signal of enchanting music, the throng of capering figures breaks like the waves of the sea, allowing this young Venus to come forth and float over the boards in a solo; if one can call it a solo, when a thousand hearts are tripping in unison with her.

Now, with as great pleasure as Milton quitted the lower regions, I can now return to Covent Garden and Drury Lane and make good some omissions. Pray excuse these sudden transitions, my friend: I venture to make them, taking comfort from the thought that among my many promises to you, I certainly did not guarantee

[1] Giovanna Baccelli, died 1801. She was kept by the Duke of Dorset: her portrait was painted by J. Roberts, by Gainsborough, and by Reynolds. The Reynolds portrait is the best known, through J. R. Smith's engraving.

to write of everything in its proper order. I saw Macklin, who is well known for his extraordinary excellence, his lawsuit,[1] and his physiognomy, play Shylock in Shakespeare's *Merchant of Venice*. You know that Macklin as Shylock sounds as well on a playbill as Garrick as Hamlet. It was on the very evening that he played again for the first time on the conclusion of his lawsuit. When he came on the stage, he was thrice greeted with general applause, which on each occasion lasted for quite a quarter of a minute. It cannot be denied that the sight of this Jew is more than sufficient to arouse once again in the mature man all the prejudices of his childhood against this race. Shylock is not one of those mean, plausible cheats who could expatiate for an hour on the virtues of a gold watch-chain of pinchbeck; he is heavy, and silent in his unfathomable cunning, and, when the law is on his side, just to the point of malice. Imagine a rather stout man with a coarse yellow face and a nose generously fashioned in all three dimensions, a long double chin, and a mouth so carved by nature that the knife appears to have slit him right up to the ears, on one side at least, I thought. He wears a long black gown, long wide trousers, and a red tricorne, after the fashion of Italian Jews, I suppose. The first words he utters, when he comes on to the stage, are slowly and impressively spoken: 'Three thousand ducats.' The double 'th' and the two sibilants, especially the second after the 't', which Macklin lisps as lickerishly as if he were savouring the ducats and all that they would buy, make so deep an impression in the man's favour that nothing can destroy it. Three such words uttered thus at the outset give the keynote of his whole character. In the scene where he first misses his daughter, he comes on hatless, with disordered hair, some locks a finger long standing on end, as if raised by a breath of wind from the gallows, so distracted was his demeanour. Both his hands are clenched, and his movements abrupt and convulsive. To see a deceiver, who is usually calm and resolute, in such a state of agitation, is terrible. The play was followed by an afterpiece, *Love à la Mode*, of which Macklin is the author. He plays, moreover, the part of Sir Harry Macfarcason [*sic*][2] quite inimitably, scarce ever going off the stage (probably because he is the author).

[1] Macklin had a lawsuit against certain men, who, jealous of his success, conspired to hiss him off the stage at a performance of *Macbeth* on 18 November 1773. After a long and complicated lawsuit they had to pay costs and a considerable sum as compensation. [2] Sir Archy Macsarcasm.

It is most entertaining and abounds in witty sallies. I have also seen this same player as Macbeth, in the part that gave rise to the uproar which was the cause of the lawsuit. I cannot say that I found him particularly pleasing, although he played with great understanding; unfortunately this man has not only the years, but the stiffness, of old age. I am always grieved to see an old actor fall down on the stage, since I am aware that he, too, must be deeply grieved.

I believe (I should say, rather, I fear) that I shall write to you yet again. My fellow traveller has grown worse during the last three days. Farewell.

London.
2 December 1775.

LETTERS

LETTER 1

To CHRISTIAN GOTTLOB HEYNE[1]

London, 17 April 1770.

Honoured Sir,

A week ago, after a very toilsome journey of fifteen days, I reached this enormous city in better health than I thought to be. It is incredible how great an impression has been made on me by the quantity of fresh objects, which my head could scarcely hold at first sight. One thing was constantly driving another out of my mind, and I am still living in such a state of confusion that I, who could usually fill pages with all the small happenings of the town, am perplexed how to reduce to clear outlines enough of London and of the confused mass of things I might relate to fill even a short letter. I have seen the sea, several men-of-war of 74 guns, the King of England in all his glory with his crown on his head in the Houses of Parliament, Westminster Abbey with its famous tombs, St. Paul's, the Lord Mayor, proceeding with great pomp through a mob of several thousands, all crying 'Huzza, God bless him, Wilkes and liberty'; all this, moreover, in one week. As your Honour can well believe, these varied happenings must be to a spirit as retired as mine what a week of gaudies and wedding-feasts without repose or sleep would be to my body. Moreover, I am living here in a house where I have neither time nor peace to collect my thoughts; as at court, I have to dress twice a day, and I dine at half past four and sup at half past eleven, usually in a large company. If one goes out, the distractions in the streets are even greater, and the monstrous all-pervading din, the multitude of fresh objects wherever one looks, the throng of coaches and human beings, are generally cause enough to make one late or even to prevent one from reaching one's destination. This has lately been my experience; I went out with the firm resolve of waiting on Herr Dieterich's correspondent in the Strand; but, before I could get there, my attention was so much caught by silversmiths, shops

---

[1] Christian Gottlob Heyne, 1729–1812. Born at Chemnitz, studied at Leipzig University, classical scholar, archaeologist, and philologist. After a varied career he was, from 1763 until his death, Professor at Göttingen.

of Indian wares, instruments, and the like, that I scarce had time to return home in time to dress, and on this expedition did not succeed in reaching Mr. Elmsley's[1] house. Those places which I have seen I visited in Lord Boston's[2] coach and in his company, or else I might still be lying in some inn between here and St. Paul's. Since I shall probably be returning to Göttingen with the young Adams,[3] and earlier than I had expected, I will keep all descriptions of what I have seen until then. I should like to remain here, but assuredly in other circumstances than my present ones. They have taken me up and shown me such consideration as I had in no wise expected; but I have had to accustom myself to a style of living which I can never maintain in the future and it is indeed too late for me to learn, so that it is quite odious to me. If I began to be charmed with it, I should be completely lost. It would be infinitely more agreeable to me if I could live more to myself and on a lower scale, even if I had to purchase this good fortune by offices which at home I should not undertake. I already have several very respectable friends here, among whom I can count Lord Marchmont, who lately conversed with me in public in the Houses of Parliament, and the next day waited on me quite alone in my room; but I dare not make any such proposal, since it would certainly deeply offend honest old Lord Boston.

I conversed with Lord Marchmont[4] on all manner of subjects. He is considered here to be one of the greatest statesmen and wits in England, and is also a great amateur of mathematics and physics, and has an exceedingly high opinion of Göttingen and the Germans. He is far from contented with the Royal Society here, and says that the matters discussed there are of so little importance that he could

[1] Elmsley (in the 1867 edition transcribed erroneously as 'Elmbley'). Peter Elmsley, 1736–1802, the well-known bookseller. His shop was in the Strand, opposite Southampton Street. He had a house in St. James's Street.

[2] The holder of the barony of Boston. He was Sir William Irby, first baron; the barony was created in 1761. He was born in 1707 and died 10 March 1775. He was succeeded by his son Frederick Irby who died 1825—not by the Mr. William Irby mentioned later.

[3] The two Adams brothers were sent to Göttingen in Lichtenberg's care in 1770 and studied there two years. The elder brother went into Parliament, and the younger, Charles, was for a short time in the Army.

[4] This was evidently Hugh Hume, third earl of Marchmont, who died in 1794. He succeeded to the title in 1740. When Lord Polwarth, he was M.P. for the town of Berwick; he was a noted opponent of Walpole. The son mentioned, Lord Polwarth, was created Baron Hume of Berwick in 1776. He died in 1781, when the British title came to an end.

not advise me to attend. When I asked the cause of this decline, he answered me merely with a shrug of the shoulders.

Göttingen is held here in great esteem, and every one questions me as to the arrangements there and wonders that there is no English or French description of it. I should think that this desire might quite easily be complied with. There would be no need for a complete translation of Pütter's description, since I doubt whether this would have any success with the females, who are, however, the most solicitous in this instance. If Göttingen desires to be visited by Englishmen, such a description is quite indispensable; otherwise only young officers are sent thither, for the most part for the sake of the German language, and this they forget, as well as Germany itself, since military service and their manner of living runs contrary to all their former studies. Therefore, if that University could only be visited by others, it would promote the fashion for German literature over here, were there only more Lord Marchmonts; though he does not even understand German, and has read only works written by Germans in Latin, being acquainted with the rest through his son's descriptions. I know several genteel females here, who would read at tea a description of Göttingen with as much eagerness as the public advertiser.

For some time a news-sheet, *The Whisperer*, has been appearing here, which is full of aspersions on the Government and the King. But here, so they tell me, little heed is taken of it, and all this is not so dangerous as it would appear to those viewing things from afar. To-morrow Wilkes will be freed, and the town is all agog to know what will happen. Some believe that the whole city will have to be illuminated, but most hope that all will pass off more quietly than on former occasions. Now I know what an English mob is. On the second day of rejoicing we found ourselves near Ludgade [*sic*] Hill, right in the midst of the crowd, which thronged several streets. They wished to welcome the Lord Mayor,[1] Wilkes's great friend, as he was driving to church with great pomp. We were sitting in Lord Boston's carriage, and it was safest for a coach with armorial bearings to pull up and act as though one had come thither for the same purpose as the crowd. The mob was enchanted to see what was as good as a state coach in its company, and I, having let down the glass, was looking out with a countenance full

---

[1] William Beckford, 1709–70, father of the eccentric author of *Vathek*, of the same name. Elected Lord Mayor in 1769. A violent partisan of Wilkes.

of curiosity. All who went past stared at the arms on the coach, cast friendly glances at me, and several cried, as they pointed at the magnificent livery and the carriage, 'There is Wilkes for you, damn me! Wilkes and Liberty, huzza,' and went on without doing us the least harm. I could not possibly describe what strange figures I saw—half-naked men and women, children, chimney-sweeps, tinkers, Moors and men of letters, fishwives and females in grand array; each creature, wild with joy and intoxicated by his own vagaries, shouted and laughed without offending any one. I think that a crowd of unruly students is much more dangerous than ten thousand such people. Often no manner of stratagem can be any protection against the former, while here any one may feel secure with an English suit and a little dissembling. I hope shortly to write further, and await Your Honour's commands. When the letter reaches me, I will carry out your instructions with the greatest exactitude. Mr. Irby, as well as Mr. Swanton,[1] desire to be kindly remembered to you, and I have the Honour to be, Sir,

Your obedient Servant,
G. C. Lichtenberg.

LETTER 2

To ABRAHAM GOTTHELF KÄSTNER[2]

London, 17 April 1770.

Honoured Sir,

Notwithstanding I have heard or seen nothing during my stay in London which could interest your Honour as a man of learning, I take the liberty of writing to you at the first opportunity. For, not only do I suspect that, if I waited for something curious to relate to you, I might perhaps never write; but also I am persuaded that you will not be unwilling to have news of my present situation, since you have at all times taken a sympathetic interest in it. On the 10th of this month I arrived here in excellent health—indeed better than that of most of my travelling companions. The journey

[1] Mr. Swanton was an officer who was conspicuous in the war in America. He studied at Göttingen.

[2] Abraham Gotthelf Kästner was born in Leipzig in 1719 and died in 1800. He was Professor of physics and geometry at Leipzig, and a brilliant epigrammatist.

lasted fifteen days, and was exceedingly irksome and full of dangers. Three miles beyond Osnabrück our coach broke down and we had to buy another, since we should either have had to remain some days in a wretched place or return to Osnabrück on foot. I spent two days and two nights on the sea, over eight hours in such a tempest that our foresail was torn, and most of the sailors were seasick, which occurs seldom. The captain was forced to sail northwards to reach deeper water, because we feared at any moment being driven ashore; so we overshot Yarmouth. It chanced that my bed stood near a porthole, through which a wave dashed in, sousing everything; a nigger, seeing this, took compassion on me and brought me another bed, notwithstanding the great tumult and that one could scarce walk a step. On the following day the wind turned, so much indeed to our advantage that in the space of sixteen hours we were able to make good our mishap, and at ten o'clock in the evening cast anchor in the harbour at Harwich. My sea-sickness lasted from ten o'clock in the morning until after five in the evening, and I was infinitely less incommoded by it than many other persons on board.

In Utrecht Herr Hennert was exceedingly civil to me, merely because I came from Göttingen, taking me up to his Observatory, which does not seem to flourish very greatly under his custody. It is situated on the western side of the town on the ramparts, and Herr Hennert lives on the east side, also near the wall, a good half hour away; but there is a small lecture room there, in which Herr Hennert sometimes lectures on astronomy, and people live in the lower floors, so it is not devoid of convenience. The tower is fairly high, and square: at the summit stands a small, round building, which has a movable roof covered with wood and lead, and round about this little circular house is a convenient space for large telescopes: in all these respects it is more convenient than that at Göttingen. They have no wall quadrant, but an excellent transit-instrument, and a special instrument for corresponding altitudes of the sun, made with great skill by an Englishman, an azimuth quadrant, and another $2\frac{1}{2}$ feet high, which can also be used for surveying, as well as a quantity of small instruments of Musschen-broek. Professor Hahn was not at home, and I had not time enough to wait upon him twice at his remote house. Utrecht and The Hague are such fine towns, of an aspect to me quite new and unusual, so that I felt myself there amply repaid for the many jolts and discomforts in Westphalia. I passed through Leyden by canal at three o'clock in the night; I was unable to stop the boat, but had myself waked and was sensible of a strange emotion at passing so silently through one of the most famous cities in the world. I saw the summits of some magnificent buildings outlined against the clear sky, and heard a chime of bells; and thus I beheld *Lugdunum Batavorum*.

Lord Marchmont, Lord Polwarth's father, a great admirer of the Germans, sought me out in my room. Not even in Germany have I seen a more ardent admirer of Wolff[1] than this nobleman, for, when I lately attended a sitting of the House of Lords, he entered on the subject of Wolff, although it was our first meeting and we only had a few minutes' conversation. He was amazed, he remarked somewhat scornfully, that the Germans invented so many things which the English could not imitate, and he instanced Winckler[2] and electricity and Störck[3] and his hemlock. The fashion for German literature would be infinitely advanced in England if there were many more such Lords. He assured me that the much vaunted accuracy of Harrison's[4] timekeeper was probably a mere chance, and could scarce find words to describe what wretched people English artificers generally were in matters of theory. He cannot conceive how they contrive so excellently to construct machines, which they nevertheless often explain and understand quite incorrectly. One machine alone did he praise, and this I shall visit. I have not yet seen Mr. Demainbray[5] because he lives in Richmond, which I cannot visit until next week. Here

[1] Probably refers to Christian Wolff (1679–1754), chancellor of the University of Halle. Famous as a rationalistic philosopher. Several of his works were translated into English.

[2] Johann Heinrich Winckler, Professor of physics in Leipzig; born 1703, died 1770.

[3] Anton van Störck, doctor of medicine, councillor and director of the General Hospital in Vienna; born 1731. He wrote in 1760 an interesting treatise on hemlock.

[4] John Harrison, the noted horologist, died 1776. He won a prize offered by the Government for the discovery of the method of determining longitude at sea. The King was personally interested in Harrison, and one of his chronometers was placed in the King's private observatory at Richmond.

[5] Demainbray, Stephen Charles Triboudet, 1710–82, the astronomer and electrician. He was a pupil of Desaguliers. He was tutor of George III. Demainbray held many appointments, including that of Astronomer at Kew, where his son Stephen, B.D. of Exeter College, Oxford, succeeded him. Stephen Peter Rigaud of Exeter College was related to him. This was the Savilian Professor and Radcliffe Observer.

I have to live too much with people of quality to be able to learn much, and I would give much to live in London in the same obscurity as in Göttingen. However, I am forced to dress twice a day in different costumes, to live and eat in numerous society, and to accustom myself to new modes of living, which I never can or will keep up on the other side of the Channel.

I saw the King in his crown in the Houses of Parliament, and also St. Paul's Church, Westminster Abbey, Carlton House, the Palace of the Princess of Wales, and yesterday I was at the British Museum and received a ticket to view it next week. I shall not probably remain here very long, and on my return will give your Honour a more particular description of all I have seen. In the meantime I await your Honour's commissions and will execute them with the greatest precision if I am still here.

I beg leave to present my humble respects to Mr. Baumann; if it is possible, I will bring a good piece of crown and flint glass with me.

I have the honour to be, Sir,
Your most obedient Servant,
G. C. Lichtenberg.

LETTER 3

To JOHANN CHRISTIAN DIETERICH[1]

London, 19 April 1770.

Dear Friend,

I am infinitely obliged to you for your security; you are a friend in need, and of such I have had but few. I hope to return soon, since I do not profit by my stay here as I had thought to, notwithstanding I live in such a way as would enchant a Darmstadt head-forester,[2] and I could wish each fat honest fellow who travels for the sake of eating and drinking nothing better than to be in my place. In short, I am living (against the grain, that's the worst of it) like a duke, and am convinced that if I continued to live in this

[1] Publisher and bookseller in Göttingen, born 1722. Lichtenberg lived in part of Dieterich's house. A bond of close friendship between them and their families existed. Dieterich outlived his friend only till June 1800.

[2] Darmstadt head-forester. This refers to a character in a novel which Lichtenberg planned, but never wrote. Cf. *Nachlass*, p. 12.

style throughout the summer, my tastes might become tuned above
concert pitch and make an everlasting discord with my purse. It
is said that the Englishman feeds simply, which is true in the sense
that one sees few made-up dishes, but they have such a quantity
of plain things that it would be sheer folly to partake of all. The
variety of their wines is inexhaustible. One first eats the midday
meal, and then comes the midday wine-drinking, two entirely
different ceremonies. At the latter no females are present; this for
various reasons, first, that they may not worm state secrets out of
the men, and secondly, that their own secrets be not stolen. All
meet again at tea, but this does not last long, and each sex does its
best to keep its thoughts to itself for this short time. In the evening
—or rather night, as we Germans should call it—things are no
better; that is to say, as far as eating and drinking are concerned,
for it is most decidedly worse for keeping secrets. I assure you that
one is in a pitiable state and cannot even think of tea-drinking. In
London everything is cheap which in other lands cannot be bought
for untold gold, and indeed one can have it gratis, all pell-mell at
any hour of the day in any street, got up in any way you like,
dressed, bound up, hitched up, tight-laced, loose, painted, done
up or raw, scented, in silk or wool, with or without sugar; in short,
what a man cannot obtain here, if he have money, upon my word,
let him not look for it anywhere in this world of ours, not even in
the good old days of our grandfathers. Generally I do not care to
write about females, and I scarcely ever do it, if the female of the
man to whom I am writing, or he himself, be not something out of
the common. Here is a case where the cap fits both, so for once in
a way I will write concerning females till I am tired of the subject.
The moment one sets foot in England (but I presume that one has
something more than feet!) the student, as well as the philosopher
and bookseller, is immediately struck with the extraordinary
beauty of the females; and the number of these charmers increases
the nearer one gets to London. I know only one remedy for a man
who is not quite sure of himself in this respect: to take the next
packet back to Holland, where he will be safe.

I have seen many beautiful females in my day; but since I
reached England I have seen as many as in all the rest of my life
together, and yet I have only been in England ten days. Their
remarkably pretty costume, which would set off a Göttingen fruit-
seller, adds to their charms. The housemaid who daily lights my

fire and warms my bed (with the warming-pan, of course, my friend) comes into the room now with a black and now with a white silk hat and a kind of train, carrying her warming-pan with as much grace as many German ladies would a parasol; in this garb she kneels down before the bed with such nonchalance that one would think she had forty such trains; and speaking an English that may scarce be found in your best English books, my friend. If your heart be not too susceptible, come over here, and I can vouch for it that you will have no difficulty in understanding their English before the bed has been warmed forty times.

The streets swarm with these creatures, of whom the prettiest are the milliners, as the English call them; it was one of these females who cost Lord Baltimore[1] 120,000 thalers, and there is yet another species of them, of whom I can say nothing beyond the fact that they have never been known to put a man to the expense of 120,000 thalers. In short, the *poenitere*, which was once valued for Demosthenes so inordinately high that he could not purchase it, is cheaper here than in the whole world.[2] If you do not understand this learned passage, get some one to explain it to you. Here I have found it impossible to be at the same time modest and plain.

I have seen over two hundred ladies of quality together in one chamber at the House of Lords; only think, two hundred, of whom each would have been worth at least 150,000 thalers to Lord Baltimore; that would make 200 times 150 thousand—that is thirty million thalers—for the females themselves in the state in which God created them, not to take into consideration the least fragment of diamonds and lace, pearls and the like. What a sum! But now I am indeed weary of writing concerning Englishwomen, and I think that when, like myself, a man cannot remain here longer, it is on the whole better to gape at them than to write. In the meantime I beg you will not insert this account of English females in the Gotha Calendar, not on my own account, but for the sake of the German females. One can sing the praises of the ladies of Lima as long as one desires, but the English females are somewhat too near them. One reads in history that the men of Lower Saxony once crossed over to England in hordes, and weighty political

[1] Frederick, sixth and last Lord Baltimore, 1731–71, a man of curiously chequered career, and the owner of Maryland.
[2] This anecdote is told by Gellius, *Noctes Atticae*, i. 8. 5.

causes are instanced as the reason for it; but this is not in the least necessary; the good Saxons were simply running away from their wives. So not a word of my description must find its way into the Calendar.

I have distributed widely your plans for subscription and will see what comes of it. Mr. Backhaus's account amounts, so they say, to some 160 thalers, not 80.

Forgive the vast deal of jests I have written in this letter. When I have the honour of seeing you again, you shall hear everything, for, as I said, it is just as difficult to be modest and plain as it is to be complete and brief. In an hour I am going to the Tower. Two nights ago many streets were illuminated on account of the liberation of Wilkes, but, without any particular uproar, Wilkes has gone into the country. He considers it beyond dispute that he is a Member of Parliament, and will soon desire to take his seat: but, if he does this, great disturbance will be caused, since it has been decided in that case to take him forthwith to Newgate, the common jail. I beg leave to present my humble respects to Frau Dieterich and the two gentlemen.

Mr. Swanton will be mounting guard until Thursday. Do not show this letter to all and sundry. I am, dear Sir, with great regard, your friend and servant, G. C. Lichtenberg.

Just as I am closing my letter, the King has sent his groom of the chamber to me, bringing me word that he has given his astronomer special orders to show me everything with particular attention, and that for this purpose I am to betake myself next Sunday to Richmond.

LETTER 4
To DIETERICH
London, 30 September 1774.

My dear Dieterich,

At last I send you a letter from London. I set foot in England last Sunday at 3 o'clock in the afternoon and on the following Tuesday at half past four I made my entry into London. On the sea I was not really indisposed, but the tossing of the ship occasioned such a loss of appetite as, still continuing, weakens me greatly, so that yesterday I called in a physician on that account. Lord Boston is in the country 28 miles distant, but my lodging was all ready for me, and for some days I played the master of the house; but yesterday, desiring company, I moved at Sir Francis's invitation to his house, where I dined, breakfasted, and drank tea in this most respectable family with two of the most lovely females in London. My journey was far from comfortable. In Osnabrück I had the devil's own luck and had to lie there for four days. This time I passed very quickly through Holland.

I have already seen plays in both playhouses, in one *Love in the Country*, not that of Weiss, but an English love in the country, in which a certain Miss Catley[1] sang wonderfully sweetly. They say that she plays 'love in the town' on her own account just as well, and it is not known whether the stage or the bedchamber be the more profitable. Some weeks ago the King and Queen breakfasted with Lord Boston, and both inquired after me. This week I shall wait on no one, but shall certainly begin next Monday.

I hope that all has gone well with the printing,[2] though I am now far from content with the whole thing, and would gladly be quit of it all. The preface and dedication were begun in Hanover, continued on the Schützenkrug behind Rehburg, and concluded in Osnabrück. Heaven knows how it has turned out. I do not know when I shall return, and in the meantime I have seen, heard, and done a vast deal. But I am still too dizzy to be able to write anything about it. I desire my best compliments to all your household, Professor Baldinger, his dear wife, Herr Dumont,[3] Herr Boie, my cousin, and all my friends. Of my other acquaintances, beyond Irby and Sir Francis, I have only conversed with Mr. Lemon, whom I met at Drury Lane, the others being all in the country. Remember me to Herr Sprengel[4] and to the Englishmen. Adieu.

G. C. Lichtenberg.

Tell my brother that I intend to send him a long letter by the next post.

---

[1] Miss Catley, 1745–89, the beautiful and clever daughter of a London coachman. She first appeared in public in 1762, and for some time lived under the protection of Sir Francis Delaval. She sang at Covent Garden and at Marylebone Gardens and ultimately married General Lascelles.

[2] The work, Tob. Mayeri, *Opera inedita*, vol. i, &c., *edidit et observat appendicem adjecit*, G. C. Lichtenberg, 1774, was dedicated to King George III.

[3] Dumont. A bookseller in Göttingen.

[4] Sprengel. Member of a small and select club in Göttingen, to which Lichtenberg also belonged. They met on Friday evenings for supper and talk.

LETTER 5

To BALDINGER[1]

Hedsor in Buckinghamshire, 8 October 1774.

Honoured Sir,

I write to you as soon as the giddiness will permit me, which is bound to attack any one who suddenly finds himself transported from a back-building in Göttingen into one of the first streets of the capital of the world, so that I may by my punctuality at least redeem my solemn promise of writing, which I might otherwise have omitted to fulfil. That is to say, I will endeavour to write as soon as possible, even if the contents of this letter are not worth the trouble of opening it, blowing off the sand, and reading it, as I almost apprehend. I stayed a week in London, and should have remained there longer, had not the sudden dissolution of Parliament called to town my host, old Lord Boston, who three days ago brought me hither to his romantic country seat in one of the most charming neighbourhoods in England. I quitted London very willingly, although I had as yet heard nothing of the Promised Land to which I have been led, since scarce any of my acquaintances or of the persons with whom I both desired and had to converse were in the town; nevertheless, I spent this week in London in such a way as I can say that I enjoyed London in so far as it be possible in eight days to enjoy it. At Drury Lane I saw a comedy, *The Fair Quaker*, with the Naval Review at Portsmouth, and a pantomime. Mr. Weston and Mr. Moody,[2] two famous comic actors, appeared to astonishing advantage, the latter playing Commodore Flip; he spoke, cursed, and swilled as heartily as a head ostler, which, indeed, he resembled, except for his legs. The first play was *The Meeting of the Company*, which has caused a great sensation here, and where the famous King was seen to peculiar advantage. By the way, I must tell you that *The Fair Quaker* did not wholly please me, though some scenes in it are very good. The next day I saw at Covent Garden the operetta, *Love in a Village*, in which a certain Miss Catley sang so sweetly that she almost made me

---

[1] Ernst Gottfried Baldinger, born 1738 at Erpert, Professor in Göttingen, 1773–82. Died 1804.

[2] John Moody, 1727–1812, a native of Cork, commenced life on the stage in Jamaica, later he played in London under Garrick and took a great number of parts. He was the original Commodore Flip.

forget the ——. She is a black-haired, lively, saucy creature, and has a charming voice, so powerful that she can make herself heard, if she will, above the most insistent *accompagnement* and the applause of an adoring public. The famous Shuter played *The Justice of the Peace*. Every word he uttered was applauded, but he did not please me, at least, not in this part, for I believe that he is a greater old fool than Woodcock, whom he was playing; his constant exaggeration led me to suspect this. At Foote's Theatre in the Haymarket I saw the famous *Beggar's Opera* and an afterpiece, *The Waterman*: and in Sadler's Wells I attended a performance of rope-dancing and other feats, as well as a pantomime, *Harlequin Restored*. In the latter house, where the company is less brilliant, the sum total of the pleasure enjoyed is greater than that of all the other houses together. One's amusement is more spontaneous, since less people are led thither by the dictates of the mode than is the case in the other theatres. When I arrived, it was so full that I could only obtain a seat by taking a nice little maiden of six years old on my lap; having done this, I saw everything excellently. I do not know whether anything is known in Göttingen of Mr. Cox's[1] Museum—in the learned journals of Gotha there was once something concerning an instrument that is to be found there—for I have just seen this Museum. More of that later. At seven o'clock on the morning of 6 October I climbed to the summit of St. Paul's Church and drank your health and that of your dearest wife. With my glass in my hand I called out the names of all my friends which occurred to me, on the pinnacle of the second place of worship in the world, above a dome 420 feet in circumference and raised 350 feet higher than the tallest houses of immeasurable London, below me the Thames with its three bridges, of which the highest cost two million thalers, ships, human beings, coaches, and countless houses. Imagine your friend, to whom Heaven has denied many things, but not, thank God, a lively sensibility, standing up there, and you may think of him, at this moment at least, as supremely happy.

I am living, as I said before, in one of the most delightful spots in England. The King, who breakfasted here with Lord Boston a week before my arrival, was so charmed with it that he had a

---

[1] James Cox, the proprietor of the museum of curiosities. He obtained an Act of Parliament, 8 George III, c. xli, to enable him to dispose of his museum 'by way of chance', i.e. by lottery.

mind to buy a house in the neighbourhood (i.e. Hedsor). The hills which I see from my window have some of them been sung by Pope; the morning before last I sat for half an hour in 'Cliffden's proud alcove', as he calls it; the house in which the famous Waller[1] lived is not far from here; the Thames meanders through the sweetest meadows about the hill on which our house stands; in short, I have but to open my eyes to see something which a third-form boy in the year of Our Lord 3000 would know as well as I do, such as, for instance, Windsor Castle, and the adjacent wood. I beg my respects to your dear and honoured wife, to whom I likewise address this letter, to my Dieterich and his household, Messrs. Dumont, Sprengel, Meckel, and Zimmermann. I shall certainly not be returning this year, and I should be obliged if you would let the two Englishmen and Dieterich know this.

I am, dear Sir, Your most faithful servant,
G. C. Lichtenberg.

P.S. There is no lack of political news, and every one tells me that in this respect I have come at the right time. Wilkes is really Lord Mayor. Lord North was lately set on and robbed by highwaymen near London. Two days earlier another man had been plundered twenty paces away from the same place, and on each occasion there had been shooting. I passed the spot on my way hither, and could still see the hole made by the bullet in a wall. The English highwaymen have lost their former magnanimity.

LETTER 6

To KALTENHOFER[2]

Hedsor in Buckinghamshire,
6 German miles from London.
8 October 1774.

My dear Sir,

Do not regard this missive as the letter which you, my dear friend, have the right to expect from me, for I have no time to give you satisfactory news of what I have seen since arriving in England; but I could not forbear to write a few lines to accompany the commission which I am sending you. It is from Mr. Irby.

---

[1] Edmund Waller, the poet, 1606–87.
[2] Joel Paul Kaltenhofer, University drawing master at Göttingen.

The King of Prussia met with great approbation here, and they desire to have the Emperor, as well as Prince Ferdinand, in just the same style. I have never come across any painting of the former in Göttingen, but have no doubt that one can be found there. There are certainly some of Prince Ferdinand in the Ayrers'[1] house, the best likeness being the miniature on the lid of the snuff-box which the Prince presented to the late Counsellor. It will, I fear, not be easy to get possession of it, but you can assuredly take your trouble into account.

Not only will Mr. Irby pay for everything, but I also hope that he will increase his indebtedness by taking some valuable engravings. If you will advise Mr. Schernhagen, all can be brought by the quarterly courier, who leaves towards the end of the year. The pictures must be more or less the size of that of the King of Prussia; since they need not be exactly similar, I have given no measurements, but you could make this pair to match. If you cannot get hold of the Emperor, send Prince Ferdinand alone, and vice versa. There is, moreover, no need to let one or the other of them miss the courier for the sake of waiting for its fellow. In fixing the price it would be better to leave the matter absolutely to his generosity, which in this island, as in the whole world, has its moments when it will not listen to reason.

I have been one and a half days in Holland, twenty-four hours on the sea, and eight days in London. Our crossing would have been one of the shortest—that is to say, fourteen hours or even less—had the force of the wind been as satisfactory as its direction, which was perpetually in our favour; however, it suddenly forsook us entirely, after it had been blowing with some violence. My Heinrich[2] must relate how miserably our boat was then tossed to and fro among the high waves, through which she could no longer cleave her way, for he was so greatly indisposed by this calm that he lay there like a dying man, and other passengers were in the same plight: none but we seafarers—by this I mean myself, the crew, and some other persons who had been in the East Indies— kept up, though I was sensible of some discomfort and suffered afterwards from a loss of appetite against which I am still contending. I have already fired off a few ounces of rhubarb powder to this end.

[1] Georg Heinrich Ayrer, 1702–74. Jurisconsult. Studied at Jena. Born at Meiningen, died at Göttingen.   [2] Lichtenberg's manservant.

Scarce any of the persons with whom I desired to speak are in London, all being in the country, and I too am now staying at the country seat of Lord Boston, of which I will later send you a description. I wish that I could send you a drawing of the surrounding country, which is so charming that the King, who breakfasted here some weeks ago with Lord Boston, would like to buy a country house in the neighbourhood, so they tell me. I profited greatly by the week I spent in London. I will tell you nothing of what I have seen, since I could do no more than mention the names of the places where I have been. But I must not forget to say that I drank your health and that of Professor Meister[1] and my other Göttingen friends near the summit of the second church in the world, that is to say, St. Paul's Church. Sir Francis Clerke[2] and I were together, and had brought with us for this purpose cherry brandy from a neighbouring coffee-house. Instead of a description of the prospect, you as a painter should ponder well the following data. We stood on top of a dome 420 feet in circumference, raised at least 350 feet above all the houses in London. Below us the Thames with three bridges, of which one cost over two million thalers and the others probably not much less, boats in endless succession, several hundred churches, and who may say what numbers of houses, human beings, and coaches. I have certainly often had less grains of sand in my sand-box. I must not write much more so as to spare the cover. I must, however, tell you that I am unlikely to return this year, and how early in the next I do not know. I desire my best compliments to Professor Meister and such of my other friends as you may see.

I have the honour to be, Sir, your most faithful friend and servant,

G. C. Lichtenberg.

Sir Francis and Mr. Irby, the only ones of your friends here to whom I have spoken, desire to be most kindly remembered to you.

I have just read in the journal that Wilkes has become Lord Mayor.

[1] Professor of mathematics; Lichtenberg was a pupil of his.
[2] Formerly one of Lichtenberg's pupils in Göttingen.

LETTER 7

To JOHANN CHRISTIAN DIETERICH

Hedsor in Buckinghamshire, 13 October 1774.

My dear Dieterich,

I do not know what to think. It is to-day the 13th of October, and I have as yet had no news from Göttingen. You cannot have omitted to write for lack of my address, since, as every one must know, my direction could be inquired for at the German Chancery. If I do not soon receive letters from thence, I shall not write again to any one. I assure you that it is unpardonable to keep me waiting thus. If you in Göttingen desire no news of me, I desire none of you, for I know, to be sure, that you are safe and sound; I ought, indeed, to be delighted if you were persons of such perfection that an early call to Heaven might be apprehended. But, 'pon my honour, if you are left in the land of the living until you are worthy of Heaven, you will still be standing gossip for our grand-children.

I could write a vast deal, but have no desire to do so. One commission only. Mr. Irby would like to take in a German newspaper; I should think that the *Neue Hamburger Zeitung*, or the *Wandsbecker Bothe* would be the best, so take them in for him and send them over every week. He will pay a guinea for them. Now mind you make as great haste as possible, there's a good fellow.

I have been three times at the races. Next week I am going to Windsor and then on to Cambridge, so that I shall certainly not be in London under three weeks.

Irby's direction is: To The Honourable Mr. William Irby,
Lower Grosvenor Street,
London.

Herr Schernhagen[1] will see about the letters.

Adieu, I am,
Your
G. C. Lichtenberg.

---

[1] Johann Andreas Schernhagen was 'Klosterregistrator' and later secretary to the Privy Council in Hanover. He was a close friend of Lichtenberg's.

LETTER 8

To JOHANN CHRISTIAN DIETERICH

Kew, 30 October 1774.

My dear Dieterich,

You will see from the above that I am staying in the place where the Royal Family is in residence. Not only am I living in the place, but in a Royal residence with Prince Ernst, and am eating at a Royal table with no one but Frau von Hagedorn,[1] the present intimate of the Queen, and Count von Lassberg. Every day I spend several hours with the King and Queen, and have received permission to remain here as long as I please, to go to Town or into the country and then return here, to make use of the Observatory; in short, I am perhaps in many respects one of the most fortunate of the King's subjects. Four days ago I presented to him the works of Mayer, and he was greatly charmed with them. Now I will tell you what the King said of your printing, in his own words: 'That is excellent printing, worthy, indeed, of the man's writings,' he said immediately he opened it, 'as good as Baskerville.'

At this point, as you may guess, I began to sing your praises, told of your experiments, and said that I wished I could learn how Baskerville glazes his paper. Whereupon he said, after some reflection, 'Perhaps I can procure this knowledge for the man.' I believe, Dieterich, that the King has now formed an impression of you that is so much to your advantage that you must not let this opportunity slip. Send the Pindar as soon as possible—the King wishes to see it—and the French Almanach of the Muses: you will not be out of pocket by it in the end. If only you were here in person!

I have just returned home again from the royal residence. I spent two and a half hours in a room where no one was present but the King, the Queen, Prince Ernst of Mecklenburg, Lady Effingham, and, for part of the time, a female with Prince Adolphus in her arms. I will wait until I can tell you in person what I have seen here and how much honour has been done me, for I have now little time for descriptions.

---

[1] Frau von Hagedorn, a lady-in-waiting, who had come to England with Queen Charlotte on her marriage. Her name would doubtless be forgotten, were it not for the fact that, on her retirement in 1786, she was replaced by Fanny Burney.

Now, to come direct to our business: I was delighted with the book, except in this respect, that the lune and the triangle have been broken up by the bookbinder. This is an unfortunate oversight and must certainly be remedied, if you are having any more bound. I told you, as you may remember, that a format of that particular size was chosen largely on account of the lune, and if it is broken up, my whole purpose will be defeated, as you can see. Be so kind as to send copies—well chosen ones, moreover—to Lambert and Bernouilli in Berlin, Röhl at Greifswald, Ljungberg at Kiel, Pater Hell in Vienna, de la Lande in Paris, to Niebuhr, my brothers, and Mayer's widow. With every copy write to say that it was sent at my request.

Good Heaven, had I but the time and patience to write, what a vast deal I would and could tell you. On the occasion of my former visit I saw a great deal, but in these five weeks, twice as much as during the four I spent here then. I have seen Garrick play, been three times at the races, up St. Paul's Church tower, at all the playhouses, and I have seen Mr. Cox's Museum and the Lectures upon Mimickry, something quite new. I have visited Windsor, with its famous castle, and Eton, and, dressed in an old suit, walked about in Covent Garden in the midst of a rabble intoxicated with patriotism, one faction of the mob crying *Vivat*, while the other half flung dead cats instead of *Pereats*. I have had great adventures, which I will not, however, relate, because some things cannot be expressed. I have eaten pineapple and paid six Mariengroschen for a pear, was in the hands of the *Chirurgus*, because I am in the same old world even in London.

You are wondering when I shall be returning? Some time, I suppose. . . . There is only one commission which I beg of you to execute without delay. A short time ago the Queen told me that she would like to have the Göttingen journals, and, as I was taking leave, she once more told me not to forget; so it would certainly be expedient to send over to me at the first opportunity such of this year's issue (1774) as are already out. If Mr. Partz is informed that it is for the Queen, he will certainly be glad to enclose them in the packet, and then whatever comes can be forwarded to me, as long as I am in England. Discuss the matter with Councillor Heyne, to whom I will write myself as soon as possible.

Adieu, my dear man; your old and faithful friend desires to be most kindly remembered to Christelchen and all your dear children, as well as to Baldinger and the wife of his bosom and our friend Dumont. Has Boie returned to Franckenfeldt?

I am Thy
Lichtenberg.

Do not forget to submit to Councillor von Hinüber[1] something from your press, giving him to understand that the King admired your work extremely.

LETTER 9

To BALDINGER[2]

Kew, 10 January 1775.

My dear Sir,

Your amiable communication has freed me from a veritable burden of apprehension, caused by your silence, and truly delighted that I have, as it were, again found so worthy a man, I sit down to answer your letter first of all the vast number which the east wind wafted hither to me last Saturday. I am still in foggy Kew, as sole occupant of a royal dwelling, sleeping between royal sheets, drinking royal Rhine wine, chewing at least twice a week royal roast beef. I inhabit a corner room of the house, one window facing east and two south. From the former I look out on a wide grassy common, called Kew Green, surrounded partly with royal, and partly with other buildings. In the summer vast numbers of persons of either sex walk here and enjoy the fresh air, but at present there is nothing to be seen but a few horses and boys, who romp about there, and now and then an English . . . dog's wedding. On one side towards the north, where the green is more open, I see the Thames, which at this point begins to have strong tides; and Brentford, famed for the Middlesex election,

[1] Carl Heinrich von Hinüber, 1723–92, since 1752 in the service of the English royal house, first as tutor and then secretary to the German Chancery in London. In 1768 made Geheimer Justizrat.

[2] Ernst Gottfried Baldinger—see note, Letter 5. In the earlier edition of the Letters (7. 59) this letter was incorrectly addressed to Boie. Lichtenberg completed this letter on 24 January and added two postscripts, the second on 29 January.

the Reverend Mr. Horne,[1] and the uproar and murderous deeds
that occurred there in 1768 over 'Wilkes and Liberty'. The
prospect towards the east is obscured by the cloud of smoke which
hangs perpetually over immeasurable London, which is round
about a German mile distant, and behind this cloud of smoke,
but—ah but!—over a hundred miles away, lies Göttingen, with
a few friends whom I would not renounce even for the sake of
all the riches lying between. The two other windows look out
on the world-famous garden, directly opposite them standing a
temple to the sun, which was built by Sir William Chambers in
the year 1761. It stands on a lawn where laurel and yew grow in
wild confusion. The pillars are Corinthian, and the timber-work
copied from one of the temples of Balbec.

When the weather is fine, I pass my days most agreeably. I go
then to the Observatory at Richmond, or, when it is not very
bright, walk in the gardens. The winter here is a mere trifle, and
the gardens at Kew and Richmond are so full of laurel and other
evergreen shrubs and trees, in which so many birds sing and
flutter, that I am scarce aware of its being the season when one
drives in sledges at Göttingen (almost at the same latitude). Only
the day before yesterday I made the tour of the whole of the gardens
here. Some of the glass-houses were open, the birds were singing
in full harmony, gold and silver fish disporting themselves in their
basins, and at almost every step I saw a golden pheasant or some
other bird, now near and now in the distance, skim across my
path. At one moment this seemed to be leading to a piece of
water and then, suddenly turning, would disclose a charming
prospect or a pretty little temple in the distance. The two hours
which I spent in these romantic walks in the sweetest melancholy
passed by like so many minutes.

Such is my life when the weather is fair, but what do I do when
it is wretched? When it is foggy, Good Heaven, what manner
of place is Kew? The fogs here are not only more frequent than

[1] John Horne, 1736–1812, after 1782 assumed the name of Horne Tooke.
He was the son of a poulterer, and was educated at Westminster, Eton, and
St. John's College, Cambridge. In 1759 he was ordained and in 1760 became
perpetual curate of New Brentford. While here, he was a violent partisan of
Wilkes in all the riots and controversies of the Middlesex election, though later
the two men were on bad terms. His political activities involved him in 1794
in imprisonment for high treason, but he was acquitted amidst great public
enthusiasm. Horne Tooke is best remembered as a writer of political pamphlets,
a philologist, and as a brilliant conversationalist.

in our parts and on the Rhine, but also thicker; so that lately a
servant came headlong up against the shaft of a post-chaise, which
penetrated a foot into the horse's body. The Englishman pulls
up the collar of his overcoat above his nose and steals away, each
man according to his own humour, one prophesying, one being
converted, and another shooting himself; but what do I do?
Sometimes I sit gazing for hours on end into the fire, conjuring
up faces and forms among the coals, thinking of Göttingen and,
since I am neither a bard nor a shepherd, of nothing more high-
flown than my friends. Fortunate is he who, under so lowering
a sky, has a good conscience and is not in love, or who at least does
not love in vain; or he will cut his throat like Lord Clive,[1] shoot
himself as my neighbour did of late, or hang himself, as a pretty
young creature of sixteen years of age did last Saturday. Then
very often I get up, look at my purse, and, if things seem pro-
pitious there, take a coach and fly Londonwards for eighteen
pence; I have done this fourteen times during my stay here. On
these occasions my troubles are easily forgot, and in order to show
you that this is indeed possible, I will make you a hasty sketch
of an evening in the streets of London; I will not merely paint it
for you in words, but fill in my picture with some groups, which
one does not care to paint with such a lasting pigment as ink.
For this purpose I will take Cheapside and Fleet Street, as I saw
them last week, when I was going from Mr. Boydell's[2] house to
my lodging in the evening rather before 8 o'clock. Imagine a
street about as wide as the Weender in Göttingen, but, taking it
altogether, about six times as long. On both sides tall houses with
plate-glass windows. The lower floors consist of shops and seem
to be made entirely of glass; many thousand candles light up
silverware, engravings, books, clocks, glass, pewter, paintings,
women's finery, modish and otherwise, gold, precious stones,
steel-work, and endless coffee-rooms and lottery offices. The
street looks as though it were illuminated for some festivity: the
apothecaries and druggists display glasses filled with gay-coloured

[1] Robert Clive, 1725–74, the great statesman and soldier who established
British supremacy in India. Created Baron Clive in 1760. Died by his own
hand on 22 November 1774, at his house in Berkeley Square, which was de-
molished in 1937. Clive did not cut his throat, but probably took poison.
[2] No doubt the well-known engraver and print seller, John Boydell, 1719–
1804. He formed a famous Shakespeare collection and built a Gallery in Pall
Mall for its exhibition.

spirits, in which Dieterich's lackey could bathe; they suffuse many a wide space with a purple, yellow, verdigris-green, or azure light. The confectioners dazzle your eyes with their candelabra and tickle your nose with their wares, for no more trouble and expense than that of taking both into their establishments. In these hang festoons of Spanish grapes, alternating with pineapples, and pyramids of apples and oranges, among which hover attendant white-armed nymphs with silk caps and little silk trains, who are often (here's the devil to pay) too little attended. Their masters wisely associate them with the cakes and tarts, to make the mouth of even the most replete water, and to strip the poor purse of its last shilling but one; for to entice the hungry and rich, the cakes and their brilliant surroundings would suffice. All this appears like an enchantment to the unaccustomed eye; there is therefore all the more need for circumspection in viewing all discreetly; for scarcely do you stop than, crash! a porter runs you down, crying 'By your leave', when you are lying on the ground. In the middle of the street roll chaises, carriages, and drays in an unending stream. Above this din and the hum and clatter of thousands of tongues and feet one hears the chimes from church towers, the bells of the postmen, the organs, fiddles, hurdy-gurdies, and tambourines of English mountebanks, and the cries of those who sell hot and cold viands in the open at the street corners. Then you will see a bonfire of shavings flaring up as high as the upper floors of the houses in a circle of merrily shouting beggar-boys, sailors, and rogues. Suddenly a man whose handkerchief has been stolen will cry: 'Stop thief', and every one will begin running and pushing and shoving—many of them not with any desire of catching the thief, but of prigging for themselves, perhaps, a watch or purse. Before you know where you are, a pretty, nicely dressed miss will take you by the hand: 'Come, my Lord, come along, let us drink a glass together', or 'I'll go with you if you please'. Then there is an accident forty paces from you; 'God bless me', cries one, 'Poor creature', another. Then one stops and must put one's hand into one's pocket, for all appear to sympathize with the misfortunes of the wretched creature: but all of a sudden they are laughing again, because some one has lain down by mistake in the gutter; 'Look there, damn me', says a third, and then the procession moves on. Suddenly you will, perhaps, hear a shout from a hundred throats, as if a fire had broken out, a house fallen down, or a patriot were looking out of the window. In Göttingen one hastens thither and can see from at least forty yards off what has happened; here a man is fortunate (especially by night and in this part of the town—the City) if he can weather the storm unharmed in a side street. Where it widens out, all hasten along, no one looking as though he were going for a walk or observing anything, but all appearing to be called to a deathbed. That is Cheapside and Fleet Street on a December evening.[1]

Up to this point I have written without taking breath, as they say, with my thoughts more on those streets than here. Pray excuse me, therefore, if it is at times harsh and difficult reading, for that is the manner of Cheapside. I have exaggerated nothing; on the contrary, I have omitted a great deal which might have heightened the effect of my picture, so that, among other things, I have said nothing about the ballad singers who, forming circles at every corner, dam the stream of humanity which stops to listen and steal. Moreover, I have only once put on the stage the lewd females who should really have appeared in every scene and in all the intervals. Every ten yards one is beset, even by children of twelve years old, who by the manner of their address save one the trouble of asking whether they know what they want. They attach themselves to you like limpets, and it is often impossible to get rid of them without giving them something. Often they seize hold of you after a fashion of which I can give you the best notion by the fact that I say nothing about it. On that account the passers-by never look about them, and that is 'liberty' and 'property'. As long as this is a novelty one laughs at it, especially since most of them are dressed as fine as Christmas puppets and, if they wish and can get a hearing, are a hundred times more animated than many of our living and genteel Christmas puppets; but as soon as one grows accustomed to it and is more intent on one's affairs than on these bewitching creatures, it is exceedingly unpleasant, and I cannot understand why no one has attempted

[1] Lichtenberg's description of London streets cannot be better illustrated than by referring to Hogarth's engravings and pictures of 'Times of the Day', 'Morning', 'Noon', 'Evening', and 'Night', &c., depicting Covent Garden, Hog Lane (Crown Street), Sadler's Wells, Charing Cross, and other places. Hogarth died in 1764; London altered little between 1750 and 1780. Lichtenberg wrote widely on Hogarth, so as to expand that subject for German readers; and he treated it in an extensive and journalistic manner.

to put a stop to this evil. Some of them, though looking like young
ladies, made proposals to me which would have brought a blush
to the cheek of a young student even through a hide as thick as
your sole.

(As I was writing these lines I paused while they were drying
to sip a mixture of brandy and water, since I had a tooth drawn
yesterday; unfortunately I jerked it with my elbow and have
bespattered wretchedly one side of the sheet. Pray excuse me,
for I cannot re-write it now.)

I am by this time fairly well acquainted with the common
people and neglect no opportunity of increasing my knowledge.
To my great satisfaction I have sometimes heard Englishmen say
that they would not have dared what I have dared. When I am
consumed with ardour, digs in the ribs and oaths are to me no
more than feathers to Behemoth; I am always guided by the first
impression made on me by the appearance of a mob or a company,
and am soon decided whether I can plunge into it without danger
or not: and it is seldom that I make a mistake. Nevertheless,
I have lost a handkerchief and a silver seal, for it is not possible
for one pair of eyes to keep guard over life and pockets, as well
as to observe what is going on.

I have seen a great many English plays, in five of which Mr.
Garrick took part. You shall read my observations on this man
on another occasion. On the whole, not a single actor in either of
the playhouses can be spoken of in the same breath. In some
roles he has found very happy imitators, and in the droll, as
expressed by simple and ingenuous folk, there is a certain Weston,
belonging also to Garrick's playhouse, who surpasses him. You
can imagine how charming it must be to see these two extraordinary men on the stage together, and I have had this pleasure,
namely, in *The Stratagem*, a famous piece by Farquhar, where
Garrick played Archer, a gentleman of quality who passes himself
off for a servant, and Weston played Scrub, a real tapster at a
wretched inn where the former is lodging. Garrick appears in
all the insignia of His Majesty the lackey, fine suit, red feather,
white silk stockings, and a pair of quite unexceptionable calves
and buckles. Weston, on the other hand, poor devil, had a miserable hempen wig spoilt by the rain, a grey jacket which he might
be able to fill out if he got more to eat, and a green apron and red
stockings. He is filled with pious astonishment when he catches

sight of the gentleman's gentleman[1] (as the girl at Kerschlingröder
Feld once said), though imagining him to belong to the same class
of beings as himself. . . . Archer, who is making use of him for
his own purposes, is particularly gracious, and Scrub, being
sensible of this, does his best, when he sits down, to cross his legs
negligently like Archer; but when the latter stretches out his
silken calves as he talks, the poor devil tries to cover his red woollen
ones as far as possible with his apron. This scene and some others
between Scrub and Archer are played in such a way that there is
nothing, perhaps, in this style to excel them. Imagine, then, on
the one hand, Garrick, perhaps the greatest player of modern
times and, on the other, Weston, the only man who, as all acknowledge, surpasses him in such parts, and judge whether I can be
mistaken. Weston is a strange creature, whom nature seems to
have designed to move others to laughter without having given
him the faculty of laughing himself. I have never seen him laugh
on the stage, nor have I observed the least sign that he had any
difficulty in suppressing it; and I am told that he laughs very
seldom off the stage either: nevertheless, his form and his whole
nature are quite unsuited to grave things and he would absolutely
ruin a really serious part. Some new playwrights have even
written parts for him, and then he is truly inimitable; I saw him
in a new play, *The Maid of the Oaks*,[2] where he is again a tapster,
though in rather better circumstances than Scrub. He represents
a good honest fellow, who is certainly a simpleton, but has hitherto
performed his duties well enough; but on the day when a wedding
is to be celebrated with such pomp as could only be conceived by
the inspiration of a poet and effected by English firework-makers,
directeurs des plaisirs, and confectioners, he does not know what to
do. As servant of the house he must maintain a certain precedence
over all the other servants; he is therefore running perpetually
hither and thither with quite unnecessary and purposeless zeal,
eager to act but defeated by his own eagerness, giving an order
merely to give *contre-ordre*; all this with such an air of simplicity
and candour that one likes the honest fellow and, on the other
hand, such a consequential manner towards the polishers, lamp-
lighters, gardeners, and footmen, that one cannot refrain from most
hearty laughter. He and a certain Mrs. Abington, of whom I shall

[1] Cf. note, p. 25.
[2] See note, p. 34.

speak later, made the play worth seeing and kept it going until the twenty-third performance this winter, although without them it would probably not have survived the first performance, in spite of the magnificent scenery, which cost Garrick 9,000 thalers.

Of the actresses whom I have seen the greatest are Mrs. Barry, the above-mentioned Mrs. Abington, and Miss Pope.[1] I have not yet seen Mrs. Yates and Mrs. Hartley,[2] but shall probably do so this week. Five and a half years ago I saw Mrs. Barry as Desdemona in *Othello*; now she is playing Cordelia in *King Lear* and Beatrice in *Much Ado about Nothing*. She is a perfect beauty and a great actress; in her ninth year, throwing down her catechism and knitting, she would creep with a Shakespeare into the garret and declaim to the chimneys. If I were rich, I should pack all the German actresses that I know into a ship and take them to London, so that they might learn from Mrs. Barry how to use their arms. Her features have much in common with those of Mamsel Stock, but her gestures are more supple and her air gentler. Her height and bosom could not be better. When in *King Lear* she raised her clasped hands to Heaven and then embraced her father, I was completely carried away; for a brass farthing I would give you everything but the privilege of seeing Mrs. Barry play now and then.

Mrs. Abington was once one of those creatures whom I introduced into the fifth page of my letter with 'Come, my lord', &c. Her exquisite form so captivated one of the passers-by that, instead of being at every one's disposal, she became his mistress and was kept for his sole use. This man soon died and left her, although he had not married her, so large a fortune that she could live, and moreover in some luxury, without playing at Drury Lane; she appears, therefore, in her more distinguished parts, with real jewels which are her own. Her form and deportment are absolutely perfect, but her face is far from beautiful; there is, however, about her gestures a certain incisiveness, more French than English, which is eminently suited to the parts for which Garrick casts her. In comedy, and above all when the manners of the first circles (as they say in Hanover) are to be parodied, she

---

[1] Jane Pope. The famous light comedienne, a noted character, who attained a high position.

[2] See above for notes on the other actresses: Mrs. Barry, p. 31; Mrs. Abington, p. 19; Mrs. Yates, p. 14; Mrs. Hartley, p. 35.

is unique on the English stage. In the above-mentioned play, *The Maid of the Oaks*, she speaks the epilogue in a masterly fashion. In it she compares the boxes with the Upper House, and the pit and gallery with the Lower, gesticulating, murmuring, and whispering, so that it was a pure joy to see her. More hereafter of this bewitching charmer.

You will probably have heard from Mr. Sprengel, to whom, if I am not mistaken, I wrote of it, that I sat quite near Mr. Wilkes for several hours, gazing at him and even attempting to draw him.[1] Some weeks ago I actually conversed with the King (a thing of which few can boast) concerning this political monster. But this would take me too far afield, so I must pass on to other matters.

This year (it is to-day the 24th of January) my health is worse than ever. I have been attacked now in the throat, now in the eyes, and then the teeth; yesterday I went to London on purpose to have one drawn, so that I am now in peace at last in this respect. For some time I have been sleeping so badly and been able to eat so little solid food that I am in a wretched state, and I believe, my dear Sir, that you would scarce know my face if you saw me. Only yesterday the Queen asked what was the matter with me, because I looked so pale. It is nothing but lack of sleep and, as I said, lately of solid nourishment, for I have had to live like a child on milk and pap, and these taken sparingly. When the sun shines on us again and I can leave this damp hole, I shall mend, please God.

I will write to Herr and Frau Dieterich by this post, but shall repeat nothing of what I have written to you, so pray read these friends such things from this letter as may bear telling. I shall ask them also to do the same with their letters. In this I include Herren Dumont, Sprengel, Meckel, Zimmermann, and my other friends, to all of whom I beg leave to present my humble respects. Pray excuse my style of writing, all and's and but's, not as to one who has in this island forgot his mother tongue, but to a man who has so much to write that he cannot possibly make rough copies or compose well-turned periods.

I desire to be remembered a thousand times to your dearest wife. This letter—I scarcely dare admit it—is addressed to her also. Her own discretion—a quality rare, alas, in Göttingen!—

---

[1] The editors of the 1901 edition of Lichtenberg's Letters remark that this sketch has been preserved in Lichtenberg's Diary.

will prompt her to throw the cloak of Christian charity over those passages intended rather for the gentleman than the lady of the house. I write at random, often wantonly, heedlessly, and in too great haste, but I assure you that my intentions are always good and my heart full of friendship, especially for you and all your household.

G. C. Lichtenberg.

PS. I will send Kästner some catalogues of English books and ask him to show them to you and Heyne; they are really for Church-Counsellor Geissler at Gotha, who requested me to procure them. Do not hesitate to send me any commissions for yourself or any of your friends. Why did you not send me your book for Pringel?[1] He sent me a message by the Queen that he would like me to wait on him; just fancy how he would have received me with such a recommendation!

The revised edition of Mayer's works[2] has not arrived; you observed the blunder which arose from the correction in the sheet. I, however, did not notice it soon enough to correct it in the copies which I distributed. I wrote the dedication on the journey from Hanover to Osnabrück, and here it has met with remarkable approbation. Being doubtful concerning it, I sent it to Heyne, and he altered a single word in the second part.

Adieu, dear friend, perhaps I shall be with you again in May. Then you shall hear all my news!

Postscript 2.

London, 29 January 1775.

I am already returned to London. I re-open your letter merely to tell you that I have found the scene described above among the small pictures that are made of the actors here. Only Garrick has not got a red feather, and Weston is wearing a different wig and coat. It's as like Weston as his image in a mirror; but not at all like Garrick. Nevertheless, I have seen no better portrait of him than the one in this set of small paintings representing him

---

[1] It seems probable that the book referred to is Baldinger's *De iis, quae hoc saeculo inventa in arte medica* (Göttingen, 1773). 'Pringel' is almost certainly Sir John Pringle, 1707–82, the royal physician and P.R.S., a man of great influence.

[2] Cf. Introduction, p. xiv, Letter 4, p. 52, and footnote, p. 52.

as Abel Drugger. That is Garrick to the life. I have bought six
of these charming little things and sent them to Mr. Schernhagen,
from whom you can demand them and keep them for me. Pray
show them to Counsellor Heyne and Professor Feder.[1] The two
sketches in character as Sir John Brute, showing him sitting down
and drunk, are good likenesses, and that in which he is fighting
with the Bow Street runners tolerable. Sir John Brute is Garrick's
favourite part, although people have often attacked him on account
of this play, turning against him the very zeal with which he main-
tains it on the stage, and saying openly that his own character
could be little better than Sir John Brute's; in spite of this he
continues to play it, having represented it twice this winter, as
I saw *hisce oculis*. The play is in part most lewd, but highly entertaining on account of Sir John's character, which is represented
so amazingly by Garrick.—I have now received the packet containing the Halle Journal, and desire my humble thanks for your
intimation.

What think you of the *Musenalmanach*?[2] In my opinion it is
actually worthless, especially that thing of Klopstock's[3] and the
others after the same pattern. Could you discover a single new
image in it? There was the eternal rustling in the grove, the silver
cloud, and the oak, which we have already had a hundred thousand
times; and they think that they are making something new of it
when it is uttered in throaty tones like an oracular pronouncement
from the tripod. For that style of thing I would give the palm to

---

[1] Feder, Professor of philosophy at Göttingen. The founder of a select club
for supper and conversation, to which Lichtenberg belonged. Cf. note on
Sprengel, p. 52.

[2] Cf. note on Periodicals on p. 124. The *Musenalmanach* was the chosen
organ of the group of poets known as the 'Göttinger Hainbund'. The name arose
on the occasion when the poets forming this coterie, in the course of a moonlight picnic, twined wreaths of oak-leaves round their hats and, taking hands,
danced about the oak-trees in a grove. The chief characteristics of their poetry
were an intense feeling for nature and a slavish imitation of Klopstock, whom
they revered deeply. Lichtenberg was prejudiced against them because they
scorned Wieland, an author whom he much admired, but his criticisms of
the 'Hainbund' poets both here and in Letter 11 (to Dieterich) are borne
out by the conclusions of all later critics. He perceives the real beauty of
Hölty's poetry, and praises Claudius also, though shrewdly remarking on his
faults (Letter 11, p. 77).

[3] Friedrich Gottlieb Klopstock, 1724–1803, probably the most popular
German poet of his day. His monumental work, the *Messias*, was inspired by
Milton's *Paradise Lost*. He also wrote a great many odes and lyrics, which
served as models for hosts of imitators.

Jacob Böhme.[1] Deuce take me if he couldn't write one quarto volume after another, which not a soul could make sense of but his crack-brained initiates; and even twenty *Musenalmanachs* would not weigh as much as one quarto volume. Some poems this year are pleasing, especially some of the shorter ones and those of Hölty.[2] Whoever is 'Md.'[3] on page 214? It is just like the verses of a fifth form boy, who knows they will pass muster as long as they scan, and leaves the sense to the Headmaster. Did you ever in your life hear that some radiant object which stands high can only be seen if one mounts a footstool? The creature was thinking of the sun, as I understand from the last ray; but if one has to mount something to see its last rays, it will be standing lower than the observer, and must either be already set or not yet risen. All reasonable persons in Germany will indeed concede to him that Klopstock is either not yet risen, or already set. It is to be hoped that the *Musenalmanach* will now improve. It is my humble opinion that no odes should be inserted, unless written by people who have given full proof of being able to produce something reasonable, sober, and serious; one would gladly listen to such persons, even if they were really mad. A simpleton who becomes crazy is certainly the worst simpleton in Bedlam; while Simson[4] and Lee,[5] when they go mad, are always worth listening

[1] Lichtenberg is no doubt referring to Jakob Böhme, 1575–1624, shoemaker and mystic. His work influenced all the German poets of sensibility throughout the seventeenth and eighteenth centuries, especially the Romantics at the end of the eighteenth century and the beginning of the nineteenth. His writings had a great influence on English Quakers and Evangelicals in the seventeenth and eighteenth centuries. John Law and John Wesley learnt German in order to read his works in the original.

[2] Ludwig H. C. Hölty, 1748–76, was the most gifted of the Göttingen circle of poets known as the 'Hainbund'. He died of consumption at the age of twenty-eight.

[3] Md. has been identified as Hahn by Redlich: *Versuch eines Chiffern-lexikons*. Johann Friedrich Hahn studied at Göttingen and was a friend of Boie's, who accepted several of his poems for the *Musenalmanach*. These are very indifferent in quality.

[4] It has not been possible to identify with any certainty the 'Simson' to whom Lichtenberg refers. He might possibly be speaking of Thomas Simpson, 1710–61, the astrologer and mathematician, who was, however, eccentric rather than mad.

[5] Nathaniel Lee, *c.* 1653–92, the dramatist, whose most famous play, *The Rival Queens*, remained a favourite on the English stage until the days of Edmund Kean. In 1684 his mind became unhinged, and he spent five years in Bethlehem Hospital.

The reference is somewhat obscure; but Lichtenberg probably means that

to, like Hamlet when he feigns madness. But who are our writers
of odes? For the most part persons who know as little of the
world as it does of them. How should it be possible that those
with more knowledge of the world than these sucklings should
not find all they say vastly foolish, even if they themselves can
believe that 'they touched the stars with head held high', as the
Reverend Mr. Lange[1] makes Horace say.

G. C. Lichtenberg.

Tell my good friend Dieterich that I have received all his
letters, and that I shall soon be writing to him at some length.
As I said above, his better half will receive a communication by
this post, but I do not know whether my letter to him will be
ready in time.

LETTER 10

To FRAU DIETERICH

Kew, 24 January 1775.

Have compassion, Christelchen!

On my word of honour I could not write sooner. When I converse with ladies, I collect at my leisure as many of my wits as one
requires for the purpose, for I am aware that one has need of at
least three out of the five or six, in order to say something which
they can listen to calmly without thinking of other matters, be it
one of their fellow creatures, a buckle, or a bill of fare. But have I
had no time? No time? I hear Christelchen ask, hasn't the wretch
been sixteen weeks in England? Yes, just sixteen weeks, but for
a raw creature like me the time passes before one can say 'Prosit'
or 'Now I will give myself over to pleasure', or even as swiftly
as an evening in your company, my most honoured friend. I have
seen and learnt much, written a whole book of observations, have
patches on my coat like decorations, have cut myself thrice and
got burnt four times, and seen and heard things—Good Heavens—
only those worthy of kisses would fill a letter. Indeed, the wealth

he prefers the work of men of real talent, acknowledged to be mad, to that of
authors of 'raving odes' who wrote like simpletons.

[1] S. G. Lange, 1711–81, is best known for *Freundschaftliche Lieder*, a collec-
tion of poems in antique, rhymeless metres, written in collaboration with J. I.
Pyra. Lange's translation of Horace had been criticized by Lessing.
Lichtenberg here quotes Lange's translation of Horace, *Odes*, I. I, lines 35–6

'Quodsi me lyricis vatibus inseris,
Sublimi feriam sidera vertice.'

of material is the sole cause of my writing so little, for I do not know where to begin. I understand as little of taking care of the pence, as they say, in writing as in housekeeping; a farthing to-day and another to-morrow, a line to-day and another to-morrow, are exactly like a kiss to-day and another to-morrow, and I prefer to have as much as I want on one day, or nothing at all. I, for my part, cannot bring myself to say: 'I have seen Garrick play,' just as one might say: 'I have conversed with Gumprecht.' I would have my friends see through my eyes, and I delight in painting pictures, but, if I were to paint everything I have seen, I should go on daubing away until Easter, and yet in the end Christelchen would probably do me the honour of holding her hand before her face. In fact, I should like to know what Christelchen would do if she were here in London with her love, and I were in Göttingen. Excellent, this idea comes to me in the nick of time, and I will not let it escape without at least making use of it as my own excuse. So now you and my old crony are in London, and I in your kitchen in Göttingen. I have been writing to London by one post after another, but have had no answer, even after accusing the postmen from Helvoet to Hanover. At last after a year and three-quarters comes a short note:

Dear Sir,

I should not have written to you to-day, had I not caught cold at yesterday's ball at Soho Square, so that I am prevented from doing anything more diverting, that is to say, go to the play, to the Pantheon, or to Vauxhall. What are the savages doing in the parish of Calenberg? Good heavens, do they still wear clothes there? You people can have no idea of what it means to be in England, or else you would not be in such a hurry as to demand a letter every other year. There are better things to be done here. We do not rise till nine o'clock, when you rustics are already hungry. Then our mind is given to the ordering of breakfast, which is served at 10 and carried away at half past eleven. Next our thoughts turn to matters of dress and, after we have succeeded in making our choice, we drive either in the Park or to a milliner's. At four dinner-time approaches, and then the hairdresser comes. You will scarce expect one to think of you at dinner; O fie! who would eat roast beef and English gelées and pies and think of you and your sausages. After dinner I make tea: afterwards we drive to the opera or the play, and sup at eleven. Now I protest that one cannot write letters to you in bed, where one is otherwise occupied, with sleeping. Thus we go on from day to day! —Ah! there's the bell: Mr. B., Messrs. X. and Tz., and Miss, with Miss —— and her sister, and Lord and Lady and the Duke of ——. Deuce take the fellow, farewell. More perhaps in the New Year.

I am, Sir, Your most obedient humble servant,
Christiane Dieterich.

So that's how one goes on in England. You can see from this letter how great a regard I have for you, and you will not be angry with me, for I am not laughing at you; indeed, I am convinced that scarce one in a thousand would have answered my letters, and yet I allow you to write after a year and three-quarters and am vastly obliged to you for your letter.

What are my two little princesses, Luisgen and Fritzgen, doing, and the groom of the chambers? If the Almighty did not bestow His gifts on me with so niggard a hand, I would send you all such fine Christmas presents that people as far as the Papendick[1] would talk of them. It wrings my heart when I pass a shop full of them, and heart and purse are at loggerheads. Yesterday I was in London. Mr. Irby has promised me to send something to you and Luisgen, rather as a mark of his regard than a real English present. I do not know what it is to be. To-morrow I shall be there again, because Lord Boston is in wretched health, and I fear that he is like to set out on his journey to Heaven sooner than I on mine to Germany. He likes to have me near him, so all his children desire me to remain with him, and I shall probably leave Kew for good and all next week. It is a melancholy, insalubrious hole in winter. Yesterday morning, before the King arrived, I conversed for an hour and a half with the Queen alone. She sits by the fire and I stand near her, and must give her an account of my own affairs and those of Göttingen. I do not speak as a subject, but merely as a traveller and a cosmopolitan, when I say: never have I beheld in any Princess more affability and courtesy, greater propriety of expression and understanding, a more engaging manner of speaking, not only devoid of pride but without the

---

[1] A street in Göttingen.

least trace of forced condescension—and moreover with such a gracious countenance and general deportment. Indeed, I have never seen these qualities united in any other person. You will therefore have no difficulty in believing my words when I add— though you may already be aware of this—that by these qualities alone she has so bound to her a young and healthy monarch of warm impulses, who could have had thousands of the greatest beauties for the asking, that the boldest slander has not dared to breathe a hint of suspicion of his loyalty. You will acknowledge that this is the greatest and most honourable achievement of feminine virtue and perfection that this world can show. You have read English history, but can you recollect such an example? So far-reaching are its effects that the King does not like to see any member of his household, of whatever rank, unmarried: so they get to work as soon as possible. Some questions addressed to me by him on that score are particularly agreeable (and never in all my days shall I forget them on account of the gracious con-descension with which he put them): but I will not write of them now, since I have no time to do full justice to them.

I have to-day sent a letter to Professor Baldinger also, which he will read to you, if you will do the same by him; in this way my friends will hear more about me than if I wrote the same things every time to all of them. I do this with my brothers, so why not with my friends, who are just as dear to me.

Perhaps I shall attend a sitting of Parliament this week, and I am convinced that the Americans will then fare better than on former occasions. I shall move that all the good ones be given lovely and virtuous wives, and all the bad ones lovely and wicked wives, and that they shall have all the wine they can drink for nothing. Then they would not be Christians if they went on rebelling, would they?

So you have sold your shop in Gotha,[1] and Christelchen her civic rights? Some day we will set off thither together, and, if we only have any money, we will set up a shop at the sign of the Moor which shall be quite as fine as the one that has been sold. Let each deal in whatever he will; my choice falls on cheese and cham-pagne, while some will choose poetical annuals, others little boxes, and so forth.

---

[1] Frau Dieterich was the daughter of Mevius, a bookseller in Gotha, whose business Dieterich had carried on before he came to Göttingen.

What is Marie[1] doing? If she is behaving nicely, I desire to be kindly remembered to her. If Dieterich says you are not to do this, remember me to her thrice, and, if he gets angry, six times, and so on. Until now I have been greatly indisposed and wretched. May you live well and happy. Please to give your children my regards and a kiss, especially to those who would not esteem my regards and could not endure my kisses. Pray do not forget Wilhelm.

I am, dear Madam,

Your affectionate humble servant,

G. C. Lichtenberg.

Kew, 24 January 1775.

Now I know what Mr. Irby has sent you. The head-dress with the little horse is for Luisgen and the other for you, and this is absolutely the very latest mode in England and, moreover, the most elegant coiffure, excepting for diamonds, and there were few better to be seen on the last birthday. One costs more than nine thalers.[2]

à Madame

Madame Dieterich

née Mevius,

Göttingen.

to be inquired for in the kitchen or the adjoining room.

LETTER 11

To JOHANN CHRISTIAN DIETERICH

Kew, 28 January 1775.

All your things have met with general approbation here, which will, I hope, result in something to your advantage. A short time ago, before the things were come, a learned Englishman came into Elmsley's shop and asked whether he had any copies, for a friend of his who had seen one had said that it excelled anything of the kind hitherto attempted in England. This was, indeed, expressed rather too strongly, but you can see what they think of it. How pleasing it all was to the King I have already written to you.

---

[1] This was the cook of the Dieterich family, with whom Lichtenberg is said to have had a flirtation.

[2] Written on the cover by a strange hand: 'Mr. Irby n'est pas permis d'envoyer les deux bonnets par le Courier, c'est ce qui le mortifie beaucoup.'

I have been so greatly plagued by all manner of indisposition, toothache, sore throat, and ear-ache and sleeplessness—that I hardly look like the same creature. I can at present drink no wines nor English beer, and the beverage that agrees with me best is China mixture. I had a tooth drawn by an English dentist, for which I had to pay half a guinea.

Lord Boston is very ill, and if he does not soon mend he will have to set out on his grand tour heavenwards——

It is said that voluptuousness, evil, and debauchery have never been so rampant in London as they are at present. Not an evening passes when not only one, but three, four, or five robberies are committed by footpads, not to mention burglaries and other thefts. Dozens are hanged and batches of fifty sent off to America, but all this makes no impression on them.

A week since a certain Herr Schröter[1] from Weende waited on me and afterwards came to see me in London. Although I had never seen him before, he was a most agreeable acquaintance, for it was truly delightful to be able to speak my mind again in my mother tongue. Just fancy what my joy would be if you suddenly walked into the room.

I am living now in the pleasant expectation that the *Musenalmanach* will improve, when it is rid of raving and panting odes. I admit that there are creatures who can fancy that they hear in such lines the footsteps of the Almighty and the rustling of the cedars of Lebanon, but I pray God of His grace to preserve all good people from such fools. Nothing is more diverting than when the nonsense poets fall foul of the poets of voluptuousness, as do silly cuckoos of nightingales. You reproach Wieland[2] for having immolated youthful innocence on the altar of debauchery, merely because the man, among a vast number of meritorious works which youthful innocence cannot even understand, has written one or two somewhat loose poems which, nevertheless, betray more true poetic genius than all the odes expressing false patriotism for a fatherland, where the better party wishes the whole of the trash at Jericho. During the last ten years, while these diverting

[1] Johann Hieronymus Schröter, 1742–1816. He owned an observatory at Lilienthal, near Bremen.

[2] Christoph Martin Wieland, 1733–1813, poet, and author of several novels, much admired by Lichtenberg. His work is typical of the earlier, rather than the latter, half of the eighteenth century. He became tutor to the Duke at Weimar, where he remained from 1772 until his death.

tales have been appearing, it has not been in the least easier to sacrifice the innocence of young ladies than it was before; on the contrary, one can see every day how common sense dies on the altar of mystical nonsense to the sound of odes. In my opinion Herr Hölty is a true poetic genius and certainly a loss to the *Musenalmanach*, and Claudius,[1] too, in his way, if he were not so anxious to seem original. I believe that to write like Hölty Nature must have endowed one with talent, but to equal most of the others, one needs but to read similar productions for a month or so. Adieu——

LETTER 12

To DIETERICH

London, 15 February 1775.

My dear Dieterich,

Well, that's excellent, truly excellent, on the word of an honest German on England's classic earth. So Christelchen has another girl? Isn't she content with having brought into the world Luisgen and Fritzgen? Two nice little creatures, over whom many a man might rack his brains without getting to the bottom of the puzzle. So it's a pretty little girl. Assuredly, if I were as pretty as I am little, there would be just as pretty a little fellow at your service. I was so charmed to hear of the pretty little girl that I tried to recall my muse. But, unfortunately, I found that, though women who have waited for five years can begin again, muses who have been silent for years sing no more. I wish the little creature good fortune and every blessing, and I hope that in the 1790's there will be no lack of souls and bodies eager to bring about the fulfilment of my good wishes. But now I must return to the year 1775, which, unfortunately, gives me quite enough to do.

At last I am in my beloved London, for which I have longed and schemed and pined. The evening before last I was alone with the King and Queen for more than an hour in an exquisite little room, the Queen being covered with jewels and the King, majestic beyond description, in an embroidered costume with his order

---

[1] Matthias Claudius, 1740–1815, a native of Holstein, sometimes called 'Der Wandsbecker Bote', on account of his editing a periodical of that name. He wrote many charming poems, such as 'Der Mond ist aufgegangen', which have become folk-songs.

over the coat; this morning after nine o'clock I again had to wait on the Queen, who was in a cap and black easy gown, quite *en famille*. She sent me to Lady Charlotte Finch, the Princesses' governess, and I sat for half an hour alone in the company of one of the most highly esteemed ladies in England. This happened at St. James's, and I then returned through the Park to the Queen's palace, where I was provided with a magnificent breakfast and then shown all the paintings and apartments, and even the elephants. On my way home I saw something which still hovers before my eyes; it was white, black, and red, and addressed me, and I think it was the Evil One himself. Brother, if thou hast seen the devil, tell me whether he goes about in *paille* with a black, frilled petticoat, and looks about sixteen years old, saying with his eyes all manner of things for which there are no words in English. To be quite clear, this devil had no claws or, at least, very small ones, which he had thrust into a pair of blue satin shoes; and I could see nothing of a tail, nor of horns, though I believe he had a pair in his pocket, all ready to be slipped under the cap of the first lawful wife that comes his way.

Lord Boston is very ill and visibly failing. Why don't Mr. Irby's Journals come? And now, my dear Dieterich, here are a few more commissions for you, and pray don't forget them. I should be vastly obliged if you would send as much turnip-cabbage seed as can be packed in a letter—remember this—and, moreover, some white mulberry seed, which can be procured, I believe, in Leipzig. Pray be so kind as not to let one wait for the other, sending whichever you can get first immediately, N.B.

Never in my life have I been so plagued with aches and pains as I have this winter, and the apothecaries have already cost me more than 30 thalers. I have often wished myself dead, though I kept this thought to myself, so that neither Death nor man should hear it; this for you alone. London is the place for me. It does not please me so much on account of the variety of diversions, for they are but trifles, but for the politeness and esteem with which one is treated, if one looks tolerably decent and pays for what one eats and drinks. My former acquaintances (three or four excepted) concern themselves as little about me as I about them. They are expecting a visit from me and can go on expecting it until I land again in Holland or France; I shall not wait on them.

The morning before last two fellows came to blows at the lower end of the street where I am living; at the very start one gave the other such a mighty blow that he fell down straightway dead. I saw the dead man carried away, but didn't watch the bull-fight itself.

I lately attended one of the most important debates of the session in the Houses of Parliament. I stood rooted to the same spot from two until half past seven, missing dinner and coffee, and taking in nourishment only by eyes and ears. Last week I waited on the King twice here in London. Yesterday I visited Yorick's grave.[1] I see and hear so much that I shall be ten years digesting it all. I lately disputed in a village, Hammersmith, over the Americans with sailors, carriers, and rogues.

One more request. Pray send, if possible, two copies of the best edition of the *Œuvres du philosophe de Sans Souci*, which is, I believe, in quarto, and two of the *Mémoires de Brandebourg*[2] in 4to. Send them to Elmsley, drawing on him for the amount; they are for the Irbys. Farewell.

G. C. Lichtenberg.

I desire to be most kindly remembered to our friend Baldinger and to Dumont. Good Lord, what things I shall have to tell when I return! I run hither and thither all the day long, with all my senses wide open. Only think of it! Adieu.

Isn't this an elegant seal? It is, moreover, mounted in gold.

LETTER 13

To HEYNE

London, 6 March 1775.

My dear Sir,

I will keep my promise of writing without waiting for intelligence of the receipt of the packet or your further commands, and I will begin by answering a question which I had before left unanswered: Mr. Maskelyne[3] has not received a single copy of the

---

[1] Yorick, i.e. Laurence Sterne, author of *Tristram Shandy* and (Yorick's) *Sentimental Journey through France and Italy*. Cf. p. 86, note 2, and p. 118.

[2] These writings of Frederick the Great were published in Göttingen in 1761 and 1751. The title of the second is more correctly: *Mémoires pour servir à l'histoire de la maison de Brandebourg.*

[3] Nevil Maskelyne, 1732–1811, Astronomer royal and a mathematician of

Proceedings of the Göttingen Society, and Mr. Demainbray only the first and second volumes. I cannot understand how it happened that Mr. Maskelyne should have received nothing, since I know that a packet containing the first volume was dispatched to him. If I am not mistaken, it was entrusted to Sir Francis. But I shall soon be able to inquire into the matter, when Sir Francis, who is at present staying near Oxford, comes to Town.

You will scarcely believe, my dear Sir, with how great approbation your Pindar has been received here. Mr. Salgasse, the Prince of Wales's tutor, and the bishop of Chester are full of it. The former desires me to ask Your Honour whether you have any hope of soon finishing the Virgil. He is so full of you that he lately invited me to wait on him with the sole purpose of hearing everything I could call to mind concerning Your Honour. This Mr. Salgasse studied in Holland under the most famous antiquaries, and is considered a man of extraordinary learning. He is the only savant, of all those with whom I have hitherto conversed on this island, who has a fairly precise knowledge of our literature; he reads German and takes particular pleasure in the Göttingen Journals, which the Queen regularly communicates to him. He would, moreover, prefer less articles on medicine and more from your pen, my dear Sir. I believe that nothing would give this worthy gentleman, who has so great a regard for Your Honour, more pleasure than to receive some of your lesser works. He is intimate with the King and, moreover, an honest man, so I am convinced that this man's esteem for Your Honour will be to the advantage of all members of our University.

Dieterich has won golden opinions here by his printing, which was exactly what the King wished. He has always been convinced that the Germans could do everything as well as the English, and his only regret was that proof of this was so seldom forthcoming in England. Dieterich has now proved that German artificers have taste, which the English have not always been willing to concede to them. Even the ladies and the printers here think his printing remarkably good. I wish that the poor devil could get as rich by it as many of the printers here whom he has surpassed. All the proofs of his zeal for the honour of the University I handed over to the King personally, this being the most direct way, and

much note. His grandson, Nevil Story-Maskelyne, was Professor of Mineralogy at Oxford until 1895.

he received them with infinite condescension and special approbation. I would that these marks of favour might return to the
poor devil by this same channel, but this will not be their course;
however abundant and pure the stream may be at its source, he
can scarce hope for more than a few muddied drops.

On the 7th of last month I attended one of the most important
debates in Parliament that can be remembered. On that day, in
fact, the Lower House presented to the Upper a petition to the
King, in which they beg him to take strong measures against the
Americans and promise to support him with life and property.
The Lords and Bishops were to fill in the spaces left (blanks) in
the address with the words 'Lords spiritual and temporal'.
Scarcely was the address read than the Duke of Richmond,[1] a hot-
headed supporter of the opposition, rose and said: 'I'll sooner
part with my head and my purse than do such a thing.' He spoke
at great length with a vehemence which frequently passed all
bounds, and once, putting his hands on his hips, he advanced a
step or two towards his opponent, Earl Gower, who had defended
Lord North's former plan with great moderation, and said: 'It is
madness to speak so.' I could scarce believe that such expressions
were permitted in an assembly of this kind. After him several
Lords spoke, good and bad pell-mell, until at last two well-
matched champions took the field against each other, Lord
Camden[2] and Lord Mansfield,[3] the former for the opposition and
the latter for the Ministry: they are two of the most eloquent
speakers and clearest heads in England at present. I jotted down
a good deal of what they said, but I should not have space to tell
you properly even a fraction of it. They took up each other's
points, quoted from memory Acts of Parliament, names and
numbers of pages, and, in addition to all the most telling arguments they could advance, made use of every advantage to be

---

[1] Duke of Richmond, Charles Lennox, third duke, 1735–1806. He held
several offices and in 1765 was ambassador in Paris. He was an active and often
a somewhat violent member of the House. His varied career has been frequently
chronicled.

[2] Lord Camden, Charles, first earl, 1714–94. Chief Justice of Common
Pleas, 1761; Lord Chancellor, 1766.

[3] William Murray, first earl of Mansfield, 1705–93, the great lawyer and
politician, created Baron Mansfield in 1756 and made Chief Justice of the
King's Bench. He did not become earl of Mansfield until 1776, when he had
already had many a passage of arms with Lord Camden on the question of the
Middlesex election during the stormy session of 1770.

gained from voice and deportment, well-rounded periods and repartee, which was often excessively biting; so that it would have been no small pleasure to hear such a disputation between professors in a lecture-room over some hypothetical case. But here, in one of the most august assemblies in Europe, stood two men, of whom one (Lord Camden), though far from rich, has resigned the office of Lord Chancellor of England, while the other has refused it, and debated on a matter in which the lives and properties of millions are at stake, not to mention the possibility of a traitor's death, of which they frequently reminded each other. It was vastly impressive and moving, and all to whom I have spoken of it thought me fortunate to have been present in Parliament on that day. I gained admission by means of a special introduction from Lord Boston, who drove with me to the House in spite of his indisposition. There was an audience of about fifty of us, and some thousands, perhaps, were barred out. I stood for six hours on the same spot, missing my dinner and tea.

16 March.

This is the first day on which I have any time to continue my letter. My diversions of every sort in this town have so increased that I think I shall eventually have to renounce all letter-writing to Germany. If I lived, or had lived, with none but the *noblesse* I should think myself fortunate in all this bustle; but, since I wish to know—and have indeed made several acquaintances among them—the class of men who have little to do with the west end of the town, I am tugged wretchedly hither and thither. The men of learning believe me to be come over here solely on their account, and the others, polite society, fancy that diversion was the object of my journey. Unfortunately I take a greater interest in my intercourse with the latter, since it is a question of eating and not eating. A matter which in Göttingen can be dealt with in half an hour here sometimes robs me of a whole morning (by this they mean here the time from half past ten to half past three, between the moment when one gets up from the breakfast table and that in which one puts oneself into the hands of the wig-maker), since the persons who must be waited on live so far apart, and on the way all manner of irrelevant matters so hold up one's chief business that sometimes part of this must be postponed. Never in all my life have my legs been so active; and in this respect

I shall certainly find Göttingen too small. It is nothing out of the ordinary here to take a walk in order to buy a pencil which does not come far short of a journey from Göttingen to the Scharfer mill; and yet it is easy to make up one's mind to such expeditions, for one is sure every hundred yards or so to chance on some sight which would be worth a walk on its own account.

A week ago last Thursday I attended a meeting of the Royal Society, being introduced by Mr. Maskelyne and Dr. Price.[1] On the following Sunday I spent the whole day at Greenwich in the Observatory. I waited on Dr. Priestley[2] and he did various experiments in my presence and for my sole delectation.

The day before yesterday I dined in Pascal Paoli's[3] company. He is an infinitely lively, handsome, and engaging man. To judge by his manners one would fancy that he had been educated purposely to shine at court and that he had lived there perpetually. I expected to see a Spartan when the servant announced his arrival to the company, but there appeared before us so fine and perfumed an Athenian that I have scarce ever seen his like here.

17 March.

I have hitherto had much conversation with both their Majesties, and yesterday with the Prince of Wales and the Bishop of Osnabrück. One day this week, when all the planets were simultaneously in the heavens, I spent two hours with the King on the roof of the Observatory. I have never seen him in such high spirits. For example, as I was looking very seriously through a telescope, he jestingly held his hat over the object-glass; since I did not immediately discover the cause of the eclipse, he laughed heartily at my confusion.

Herr von Lichtenstein, the Hanoverian Chief Marshal, told me lately that Stuart, the architect[4] here, had informed him that a year ago he had presented his work to the University of Göttingen, but had as yet received no news of its arrival there. Stuart sent it by Heydinger, who has played many a worse trick than keeping

---

[1] Either James Price, 1752–83, chemist and student of alchemy, who committed suicide in 1783; or Richard Price, 1723–91, the moral and political philosopher.

[2] Joseph Priestley, 1733–1804, eminent scientist and theologian.

[3] Pasquale Paoli, 1725–1807, the Corsican soldier patriot. He came to London in 1769 and received a handsome pension from George III.

[4] Evidently James Stuart, F.R.S., F.S.A., 1713–88, the architect and artist, the distinguished author, with Nicholas Revett, of The Antiquities of Athens.

things entrusted to him. Herr von Lichtenstein thinks that if it has arrived, a few lines from thence would give honest Stuart great pleasure.

Herr Kästner has not acted fairly towards me in having portions of my letter printed without asking my permission,[1] when, indeed, I had not the remotest desire for such a thing. My news was not addressed to him as President of the Society, and it was thus entirely contrary to the practice hitherto observed to have it printed. Moreover, the description of the barometer is written in such a way as to be of use, as Alembert says of logic, only to those who have no need of it. I hope that he will never do so again. I am particularly grieved to hear of Newton's monument, such a thing being, I dare say, suitable for the Frankfort Journal, but not for the Göttingen, although quite good use might be made of it in a letter to a man whom one knows.

A few days ago I was in Richard Parker's shop of statues, bas-reliefs, and busts. I wished that I had the money to present to the Library bronze busts of Sterne and Garrick, which cost 26 shillings each. It is very like Garrick, and I was told the same thing of Sterne's. There is also a life-size one of Garrick, costing two guineas; the others are rather smaller, though two feet high with their pedestals. I have not visited Wedgwood's and Bentley's collection, which is one of the things best worth seeing in England. Mr. Irby and I often wished, my dear Sir, that you were with us, when we saw a vase or a figure which aroused our admiration: the things are immoderately dear, at least for a German, and this renders the contemplation of them disagreeable, since one sees one's own poverty in each lovely object.

About three weeks ago I came on Sterne's grave[2] quite by chance. He is buried in the same churchyard in which my bones would have to be interred if I died in London, that is to say, outside the city in the graveyard of the parish of St. George's, West-

---

[1] Kästner had printed in the *Göttingisch Gelehrte Anzeigen* of 1775 some passages from a letter written by Lichtenberg to him on 20 December 1774, which has not been preserved.

[2] Sterne died in 1768 and was buried in St. George's Cemetery, Bayswater Road. The body was removed by the 'resurrection men', but a stone, repaired and preserved in the nineteenth century, with modern rails and another inscribed stone at the foot of the enclosure, marks the spot on the west side of the burial-ground, opposite the playing grounds and vegetable plots. The stone is decaying gradually, though fortunately not stacked in the long rows of two and three stones against the walls. Cf. Diary, p. 118.

minster, where I am residing, and of which, moreover, Lord Boston is warden. Two freemasons have put up a wretched gravestone to him, in this, nevertheless, putting to shame all the wealthy admirers of his writings. It was the best, I expect, they could afford, and it would therefore be uncharitable to find fault with it, but Yorick could well have dispensed with the verses inscribed there; for he must have many admirers with more wit than these two gentlemen who could have made better for him, upon my word. I have made a copy of them, however.

I do not know whether I shall have time to answer Herr Dohm[1] by this post, and I should be very much obliged if Your Honour would present to him my humble respects and say that I have received his letter and will do my best. Dr. Maty,[2] on whom all depends—next to the statutes of the Museum—is a most agreeable and obliging man. If I have an opportunity, I think that I shall gain access to the Library of the Museum through the cabinet of St. James, in this case at least. I will acquaint Herr Dohm as soon as the matter is set in train. I have also received Professor Büttner's[3] letter and already made use of much of it, but am unable to write now. I hope he will forgive me, if Your Honour requests him to in my name.

The King lately remarked to a certain gentleman that I had a salary of about £80, that is to say, some 480 thalers. I have as yet made no remark to the King on my circumstances, although I have had such opportunities as scarce any other German or Englishman of my rank could boast of. I cannot bring myself to harass so excellent a man with another such plea, after he has spent half his day deliberating affairs of the utmost consequence, reading and hearing petitions until he is weary of them; but I shall, nevertheless, find some means of informing him either myself or through another that I have exactly £40, inclusive of the equivalent value of my license to lecture. I am curious to learn who told him about the £80.

---

[1] Christian Conrad Wilhelm Dohm, 1751–1820, was a tutor in Göttingen from 1774 to 1775. He later held various diplomatic posts in the Prussian service.

[2] Either Matthew Maty, 1718–76, or his son Paul Henry, 1745–87, both officials of the British Museum. Matthew edited the *Miscellaneous Works, Letters, and Memoirs* of the Earl of Chesterfield, published in 1777.

[3] Christian Wilhelm Büttner, 1716–1801, born at Wolfenbüttel, naturalist and historian.

Pray answer the matter which concerns Mr. Salgasse, my dear Sir, by the return of post. I beg leave to present my humble respects to your good lady, and have the honour to be, Sir,

Your most obedient Servant,

G. C. Lichtenberg.

PS. I will write by this post also to Counsellor Kästner and Professor Dieze,[1] if nothing unexpected prevents me; I have begun letters to both of them.

I have sent to Hanover the third number of the weekly journal, *The Crisis*, which was burned last Monday by the public hangman outside the Exchange and the Houses of Parliament. Your Honour can demand it of Herr Schernhagen and keep it for me, since I have the five other numbers, but pray do not allow any one in Göttingen to read it, except Counsellor Kästner. In my opinion it does not merit the attention paid it by Parliament and is not to be spoken of in the same breath as the *Letters of Junius* and Wilkes's writings. At the same time they burned another publication of the same title which goes to the other extreme and preaches despotism; it is said to be somewhat better, but I was not able to obtain a copy, since I did not hear of it until it had become a punishable offence to buy or sell it. The fact that a lampoon *pro* and a lampoon *contra* should have been burned together is, indeed, remarkable and proves the excellence of the English constitution. Every matter of moment finds its counterpoise, until one comes to the lampoon and the requital it merited.

LETTER 14

To DIETERICH

London, 31 March 1775.

My dear Dieterich,

To-day only a few lines. Yesterday at half past two my great benefactor, Lord Boston, died. It was a great solace to all of us that we had been able to foresee this for three months. He has bequeathed to the Lieutenant (as he now is) £10,000, and to young Lord Boston a fortune of £120,000, which at present only brings him in £40,000, but with care may be increased by more

---

[1] Johann Dieze, born 1729 at Leipzig, died 1785. Professor at Göttingen, and sometime Chief Librarian in the University of Mainz.

than half again. This event will tend rather to lengthen than shorten my stay in England. Now some commissions, which I beg you to attend to immediately.

Pray give my respects to Professor Erxleben[1] and tell him that a strange chance is to blame for my having delivered his letter only a month ago. A whole packet of things went to Lord Boston's country seat, and I was unable to claim it and bring it to London until I went down there myself. Now the commission has been faithfully executed.

Pray tell Dr. Weiss that I will answer his kind letter as soon as possible.

Thirdly, the Queen would like as soon as possible to have the novel *Friderike oder die Husarenbeute*.[2] Since she will in future procure her German books from you through me, you can send in your bill when several items are added to it.

Pray tell Christelchen that I am obliged to her for her pretty letter, and remember me most kindly to all your children.

A long letter to Professor Dieze is being dispatched to-day. Ask him to read it to you.

I dined lately in Paoli's company, and breakfasted with Omai the Otahitan.[3] He comes from the island where one can buy hearts and all other adjuncts with no trouble at all for an iron nail. I have sent to Herr Schernhagen a detailed account of my conversations with this acquaintance from a southern land.

Farewell, dear Dieterich.

The female modes which I sent you are cut out of this year's Calendar, and those of 1775 will only appear in the Calendar of '76. For as long as the calendar-makers are content to be merely imitators, and not arbiters, of the modes, this order of events needs must prevail. Perhaps I could discover some other means, though it might prove somewhat more costly. I should have to collect little portraits as they came out. A week ago a mode appeared which has something very striking about it; it makes

---

[1] Johann Christian Polykarp Erxleben, born 1747 at Quedlinburg, Doctor of philosophy, chemist, and naturalist.

[2] Novel by J. P. Sattler, born at Nürnberg, 1747, studied at Altdorf 1765–9, Professor of German at the Gymnasium at Nürnberg.

[3] Omai, a retainer of Queen Oberea, was brought by Captain Fourneaux in 1773 to London and was taken by Captain Cook, on his last journey, back to his native country, where he died a few years later, cf. Diary, p. 119. Sir Joshua Reynolds painted a portrait of him. One replica of it is known.

the pretty girls very pretty and the plain ones very plain, which has been the case, according to the most ancient records, in every period with all kinds of adornment. They are wearing on their heads four, five, or six big ostrich feathers, white, blue, red, and black together. They quiver at the slightest movement of the heart—that is to say, if the head can be moved by the heart—and are able to express love and hate, and *quod sic* and *quod non* and heaven knows what. All this for Madam. . . .[1]

One of the ladies to whom the feathers are not becoming.

LETTER 15

To DIETERICH

London, 1 May 1775.

My dear Dieterich,

Both I and Mr. Irby, who is no longer an officer but has sold his commission for £1,500, are infinitely obliged to you for the mulberry seeds and the journals. What wretched bungling with the Pindar, but if it arrives in the end, all will be well. How was it that my brother in Gotha received my letter of 20 December only three weeks ago?

I am very much obliged to you for the 'Sorrows, Joys and Follies of young Werther'.[2] Is it true that a young Herr von Lütichow shot himself on reading the book? What a wretched creature he must have been! I consider that the smell of a pancake is a stronger incentive to remain in this world than all the would-be powerful arguments of young Werther to depart from it. So the following might be added to the little engravings in the *Prometheus*.[3] A lover (men of sensibility best know how to depict him), and, moreover, a luckless one, stands there with a pistol in one hand and a bread-knife in the other; before him is a table with the book in question and a pancake on it, and above are written the words 'Number one', with the line from Addison's *Cato*:

'My bane, my antidote are both before me.'

[1] A part of the second quarto leaf has been cut out of this letter. It seems as though it must have contained a sketch illustrating the fashions.

[2] *Die Freuden des jungen Werthers*, the best known of all the many parodies of Goethe's *Leiden des jungen Werthers*, by C. F. Nicolai (1733–1811).

[3] Probably refers to *Prometheus, Deukalion und seine Rezensenten*, published in 1775 by H. L. Wagner (1747–79).

The other picture represents the same man; the pistol is lying on the ground, the bread-knife is stuck into the pancake, and the pancake half in his mouth, with Caesar's words:

'Jacta est alea.'

Get some one in Göttingen to puzzle out the English and Latin words for you, since I have no time for it myself.

What a vast deal I could write to you, my dear friend, if I had time and my eyes permitted, for I must tell you unfortunately that they are so bad that I had to consult one of the first surgeons about them. Heaven knows what will be the outcome, but I must await it calmly.

I desire to be most kindly remembered to all my friends, especially to your household; more perhaps shortly.

Yesterday I experienced my first thunderstorm in England; after three days of intolerable heat it gave us life, strength, and courage again.

Adieu.

G. C. Lichtenberg.

LETTER 16

To DIETERICH

Kew, 28 September 1775.

My dear Dieterich,

I have received both your letters, or the Lamentations of Dieterich! Good Lord! how can you imagine that I have anything against you. Ask my brother in Darmstadt when I last wrote to him, and he will tell you in February. Mark this. As soon as Heaven calls me to a place where my own thoughts are again my sole distraction and I must observe the weather in my head, you shall again have letters with sketches. Here this is impossible, especially since we still have a south-east wind and the atmosphere is clear.

The louts in Göttingen may say what they will, but not another line but these will they receive from me.

Pray write to me, however, about a lodging for myself and the two Englishmen.[1] The third will not be coming until next Easter,

[1] Lichtenberg escorted young Englishmen to Göttingen and elsewhere in Germany more than once, as appears by the letters.

but we shall certainly arrive in November. It must not be in your house. If it were possible to have the rooms on two floors looking on the back, and the front ones of one floor, in Thomson's house, it would do well for the winter, for I should not remain there longer (perhaps not in Göttingen). At present, however, I must return, since this is my duty, but I do so with about as much pleasure as men going to meet their death usually have. If I could bring myself to offend and provoke to anger against me some one whom I should be loath to offend, I could remain for ever on this side of the sea. Take care to whom you repeat this.

Do not take amiss the above words: the lodging must not be in your house. I have all manner of good reasons for this.

I have now entrusted my eyes to a fresh physician who was recommended to me by the Queen herself, and I hope and trust that this man will do me a great deal of good.

I shall certainly attend to your affairs before I leave. Next Monday I am going to Oxford, whither I have been invited, and shall perhaps travel somewhat farther merely for the sake of a change.

Just fancy, yesterday morning I spoke to Raspe,[1] and so greatly was he confused at the sight of me that he could scarce address me. I was quitting an assembly which he was about to join, and we met on the stairs, so that I speedily got away from him. His costume is no longer what it was formerly, and he looks almost like a ——, that is to say, what he is. That was in London, where I was yesterday and last night.

What are Christelchen and her children doing?

The morning before last two fellows had a fight below my window. I have frequently looked on at this ceremony, but never have I seen one more bloody than on this occasion. The blood of one of the fellows gushed out of his nose and mouth over his naked body and reached his arms, so that the other fellow was smeared with it, and it was, indeed, a ghastly spectacle. As they were fighting, the King and Queen came driving past in a phaeton, so close to them that part of the spectators actually had to move to the other side of the phaeton. They heeded this just as little

---

[1] This was evidently Rudolf Erich Raspe, author of *The Adventures of Baron Munchausen*. He was born in Hanover in 1737 and studied in Göttingen and Leipzig. When Librarian at Cassel, he stole gems and medals from the Landgraf's collection and was arrested, and escaped and fled to England. He died in Ireland in 1794.

as if I had gone past. One fellow was struck down by the other six or seven times and not knocked out, but he gave him such a blow on the head that he lost consciousness, sunk to his knees like a man in a swoon, and crumpled up. As soon as he came to himself, in which he was assisted by the onlookers, he ventured on another round, until the spectators interposed, fearing that he would not come out alive. Then they shook hands, put on their shirts, and each went his way. One fellow could hardly be recognized, his face being all blue and yellow, and his eyes bunged up.

Farewell. This evening I still have to write to Madame Baldinger, whose charming letter did not reach me until a very short time ago, and one of yours also. My letters now pass through so many hands that it is scarcely possible that they should be delivered speedily. Two pairs of hostile, two pairs of negligent, one pair of zealous, and one pair of genteel—*Summa* six pairs of hands. Woe is me if they must first undergo the scrutiny of hostile eyes, as I almost suspect, though I do not seriously fear it.

I could give you a few droll anecdotes for your calendar, if you would vouch for it that I shall not be had up before the Registrar's Court. So the Muses are really having their Calendar printed in Lauenburg, poor Muses.[1] Next year they will even betake themselves to the Convent at Seven.

I am,

affectionately yours,

Lichtenberg.

LETTER 17

To DIETERICH

St. Paul's Coffee House, London.

13 October 1775.

My dear Dieterich,

I am just returned safe and sound from a journey of more than 72 German miles which I made without servants, boxes, or portmantles. This evening I go to Kew, where I shall probably find letters from you. I will not wait, however, to see them, but write to you from here, since the post goes out in a few hours. If there is anything in those letters requiring an answer, I will write again by the next post.

[1] Up till 1775 Dieterich had printed the *Musenalmanach*. The number of 1776 was printed in Lauenburg.

Chiefly to oblige you, I journeyed to Birmingham, which is more than 24 German miles distant, purposely to converse with Mr. Baskerville.[1] Only on my arrival there did I learn that he was buried more than six months ago. I waited on his widow, an excellent woman, who is continuing the type-foundry but has almost entirely given up the printing-press. She lives in an excellent house outside the town, where she has also her factories, kitchen gardens, and pleasure gardens, with most elegant walks between trees and laurel hedges. The rooms are furnished with the greatest taste, and all betokens wealth displayed with that judicious moderation becoming to persons of good taste who have not inherited it, but acquired it by their own industry. She gave me six samples of her specimens of type and quoted the prices per pound. When she discovered that I was a great admirer of her husband, she presented me, taking it up from her table, with the prayer-book about which I lately wrote to you and which can no longer be obtained in London. She assured me that she had other prayer-books, besides some unbound copies of her husband's edition. If I or any one else in Germany wish to purchase type, she is always willing to send it post free to London as soon as I communicate with her, which is no trifle in this expensive country. Although she was dressed very nicely in black silk, she accompanied me herself into all the most dirty nooks of the type-foundry. I saw the punches and matrices for all the elegant letters which we have so often admired. She makes a secret, however, of the process by which the paper is glazed, though I came much nearer to an explanation of the matter by questions which I put indirectly. She glazes paper for the London booksellers, who stipulate for a particular kind of glaze, for each of which they have their own special names. Thus I have seen paper which only differed slightly from the common variety, and other paper as smooth as a mirror, some sheets of which she gave me. I enclose a piece of it. Only one young woman and a little girl are needed to tend the machine, and this pair glazes six quires of paper a day. I am almost certain that it is not done by rolling, but in quite an ordinary fashion; namely, that a smooth and very heavy body, whose nature, size, and weight I cannot determine, is passed hither and thither over it, more or less as linen is ironed in Göttingen. I have been assured by a man of learning that the Arabs

---

[1] John Baskerville, 1706–75, famous printer and type-founder.

glazed their paper in a similar way with smoothing-irons of glass. Rollers like yours are instruments intended for pressing together, and glaze only by means of the violence of the pressure, which is really their chief function. I see no reason why one should not carry out by means of one process both pressing and glazing, since the latter can be produced separately, or at least without an excessive expenditure of pressure. Another secret of which she is as proud as she is of the glazing is the receipt of her husband's printer's ink, which is unknown to all English printers. It differs not only in the beauty of the colour, but because it dries extraordinarily quickly and is absorbed by a glazed surface much better and sooner than the common variety.

Since she herself takes no pleasure in such a life and is rich enough, she is willing to sell her whole printing equipment, with all punches, matrices, and everything appertaining to the typefoundry, besides the glazing machine and the receipt for printer's ink, for £4,000, her husband formerly having been offered £5,000 for all this; she will either give 5 per cent. discount on this £4,000 for immediate payment, or six months' credit, and make free delivery to London. She has not yet advertised her intentions in black and white and not a soul is aware of them beyond her own relations and friends in Birmingham. What a chance, if only one had the money! Just fancy the type that might be cast from the existing moulds and the moulds that might be struck with the existing punches! It is a transaction which would either make a man's fortune or bankrupt him. I scarcely think it would do for Germany and, although she promised me not to be in too great haste to advertise the matter publicly, I apprehend that this will occur before we could come to any decision; then it will certainly either remain in England or go to Holland, where she has lately sold type for £150.

Besides Birmingham I also visited Bath,[1] for one can hardly say that one has seen England if one has not been in these places; in the latter town I looked on some of the scenes which are depicted in *Humphry Clinker* in so masterly a fashion.

---

[1] It is interesting to compare Lichtenberg's letter of 12 January 1783 to F. W. Herschel: '. . . Good Heavens! had I but known, when I spent some days in Bath in October 1775, that such a man (i.e. Herschel) was living there! Being no friend of tea-rooms and card-playing and balls, I was very much bored there and ended by spending part of my time on the tower with my perspective glass.'

Dr. Hornsby,[1] the first astronomer in England, who has the use of the first Observatory in the world, wishes, so he told me, for the continuation of Mayer's works more than for anything else he has hitherto received from Germany. Elmsley sold them to him for ten shillings, which is, in my opinion, too much. Hornsby received me at his house in Oxford and presented me with an excellent work.[2]

Shortly more by word of mouth.

I was interrupted while writing lately to Madame Baldinger; pray make my excuses.

I am, Your affectionate friend,

Lichtenberg.

This was penned scarce fifteen paces away from Paul's Church.

I desire my best compliments to all my friends of both sexes.

I actually spoke lately with Raspe, but not above five words.

I have a mind to write a book of instructions for Germans wishing to visit England, in the style of Rambach's[3] little book on etiquette. I have only one trifling scruple—that is to say, I should like to know whether I should be allowed to print the first precepts which I should like to have printed, if not in red, at least in large type. If Dr. Habernickel answers my question in the affirmative, you shall publish it.

You can draw all manner of conclusions from the enclosed specimen sheet. The paper appears to be washed over with something, and from the back one can see, especially where I have marked it, that it is laid on linen: though there appears to be another reason for this.

---

[1] Thomas Hornsby, D.D., F.R.S., 1735–1810. Fellow of Corpus Christi College, Oxford, Savilian Professor of Astronomy, first Radcliffe Observer, Radcliffe Librarian.

[2] Cf. Letter 18, p. 99, where Lichtenberg tells Schernhagen that Hornsby had given him some tables published by the Board of Longitude.

[3] This was probably Jakob Theodor Rambach, the Con-Rector of the Gymnasium in Frankfurt, 1733–1808. The work in question was *Katechetisches Handbuch zur Erleichterung des Unterrichts der Kinder in den Landschulen*, Breslau, 1769.

LETTER 18

To SCHERNHAGEN[1]

Kew, 16 October 1775.

Last Friday I returned safe and sound from a journey of altogether more than 72 German miles. I visited Oxford, Birmingham, and Bath. Whoever has not seen the last two places can scarcely say that he has been in England. I took this journey without servants, boxes, and even without a *portemanteau*; I went to London, laid aside all my finery in a retired spot there, and, like a journeyman weaver, with a few clean shirts and cravats in a handkerchief, took the coach and made my way back again without having been devoured. It is scarce possible to describe in a letter what I saw on this tour. I will only mention that I saw Mr. Bolton's famous manufactory,[2] or rather complete system of manufactories, at Soho in Staffordshire, near Birmingham, where 700 persons are daily engaged in making buttons, watch-chains, steel buckles, sword-hilts, cases, all manner of silver work, watches, every imaginable kind of ornament in silver, and in pinchbeck and other compositions, and snuff-boxes, and so forth. Each workman has only a very limited range, so that he does not need constantly to change his position and tools, and by this means an incredible amount of time is saved. Thus, for example, each button, fashioned in box-wood, ivory, or anything else, passes through at least ten hands. I also saw there a new kind of fire- or steam-engine, which with 112 pounds of coal can raise 20,000 cubic feet of water to a height of 24 feet in so short a time that the water by its fall sets in motion a wheel which is as large as one in the power-works at Herrenhausen. Mr. Bolton still makes a secret of it, but I managed to observe this much: the tube above is closed and the rod of the embolus is greased and fitted so exactly into the opening that the air cannot play on the embolus, although that in the London machines is propelled downwards by air alone; thus Mr. Bolton, who excludes the pressure of the

[1] See note, p. 58.
[2] Lichtenberg means Matthew Boulton, 1728–1809, manufacturer and engineer. He developed the business inherited from his father at Snowhill in Birmingham to such an extent that in 1762 he had to move it to Soho, then a barren heath 2 miles north of the city. Boulton later took James Watt into partnership and made of his steam-engine a commercial success.

atmosphere which is so necessary in the case of other machines, probably presses down the embolus also by means of steam; and this, I presume, is his secret. Since the force generated by compressed steam has almost no known limits, he can raise as much water at once as the solidity of the machine will permit. I must not forget to remind you that 112 pounds of coal delivered on the spot cost Mr. Bolton some 14 pence in Hanoverian money. I also saw an uncommon pump which raises the water in abundance, but not very high, this being effected neither by air pressure nor by steam. All this enlightened me as to why one can buy the so-called Birmingham wares cheaper in Berlin and Strasburg than in London itself. Mr. Bolton and his merchants in London, who are his sole agents in England, having agreed on a certain profit, fix a price in England compatible with this profit, so that the foreigners who buy their goods in Soho can sell them even cheaper than the London merchants, even after heavy charges for freight.

After this I saw Clay's factory for lacquered work, where the excellent japanned hardware, which is also copied in Brunswick, is manufactured, besides paper boxes, tea-caddies, and panels for coaches and sedan chairs, for in London they are now driving in paper coaches.

They make there coffee-trays of paper and all kinds of other vessels, black with orange figures in the style of Etruscan vases, which are indescribably handsome. A tea-caddy costs three guineas, but since it cannot be eaten, I could not permit myself to buy one.

From here I went to Mrs. Baskerville's and saw over the world-famous type-foundry and printing-press. Her husband is dead. She is giving up the printing-press, but continuing the type-foundry until she is able to sell it all. This lady lives outside the town in a house surrounded by gardens of which not even a prince need be ashamed; everything betokens wealth and taste, displayed, however, with the moderation of a wise merchant who won it by his own exertions. She received me with excessive politeness, and when she discovered that I was an admirer of her husband, she presented me not only with several specimens of type, of which I have already sent one to Dieterich, but also with a Common Prayer Book, printed by her husband and now becoming rare; she also entertained me with Madeira and toast.

Birmingham is a very large and thickly populated town, where almost every one is busy hammering, pounding, rubbing, and chiselling.

Bath is one of the most charming spots that I have seen in England, or almost anywhere else; here, however, I must break off, or I shall get no farther than Bath and never reach home by the end of this sheet. One other matter. Mr. Hornsby,[1] the Professor of Astronomy at Oxford, entertained me in his house for two days and presented me with a valuable work, namely, the tables published by the Board of Longitude to facilitate the calculation of the distances observed between the ☽ and fixed stars. The book is a small folio and five inches thick. This Observatory surpasses that at Richmond as much as the latter does the Göttingen one. I have persuaded Mr. Hornsby to learn German, and he will do so. Can you imagine, my dear Sir, a telescope through which stars of the fifth, and even of the sixth, magnitude can be seen, sometimes in broad daylight, for example, at four o'clock on a summer afternoon. This can be done with Mr. Hornsby's transit instrument. I had heard of it before, but thought there must be some misunderstanding, until this honest man, who is certainly no boaster, told me of it, and I had seen through the telescope Alkor, the middle star in the Great Bear's tail, so clearly at one o'clock in the afternoon that it could scarcely escape notice. When I was in Oxford the weather was not favourable enough for this, although it served for other observations. If this kind of thing goes on, the astronomers will at length be able to go to bed at night like other craftsmen. 12,000 thalers are to be spent on the Observatory at Oxford. Mr. Hornsby has already written to me, although it is only ten days since I left him.

Now something about our friend Forster,[2] beginning, moreover, with his character.

He is a man in his prime, full of ardour and courage. He would,

---

[1] See note, p. 96.

[2] Johann Reinhold Forster, a pastor and man of great scientific attainments. His intractable temper lost him posts successively in Russia and at the Non-conformist Academy at Warrington. He, with his son, accompanied Cook on his second voyage, and later became Professor of natural history at Halle. His reputation is now overshadowed by that of his son, Johann Georg Adam Forster, F.R.S., 1754–94. The latter's account of Cook's voyage: *A Voyage round the World*, London, 1777; in German, Berlin, 1778–80, was the first of his excellent travel books, which were of great importance in the development of that genre. In 1789 he became co-editor with Lichtenberg of the *Göttingisches Magazin der Wissenschaften und Literatur*.

I believe, circumnavigate Jupiter; his memory is prodigious and so, they say, is his knowledge of natural history. To his friends he is obliging and unassuming, but he is implacable when insulted, and treats his enemies with a style of witticism peculiar to himself which is highly successful, that is to say, he boxes their ears. I was told that on his journey he was twice thrown into prison. Once, because a German who was quite unknown to him was talking German fairly loudly at the play, and an Englishman found fault with this in expressions abusive of Germans in general; then Forster got up and, although he was sitting nowhere near, addressed these friendly words to the Englishman: 'You infamous scoundrel', and called him out on the spot in such tones that the Englishman, thinking discretion the better part of valour, did not show himself after the play, but slunk away. Mr. Forster himself subsequently told me this tale. His love of knowledge and zeal for truth are just as amazing, and, in short, almost the most remarkable man I have seen in England is a German, that is to say, Mr. Forster. If he had been able to command the ship himself, and had he possessed Captain Cook's experience in addition to his own great talents, we should now know thrice as much, although, as it is, the journey will not easily be forgotten.

I must now set down various things as they occur to me. They reached latitude 71° 10′, which is almost ten degrees farther than a ship ever got which found its way back again; there they were prevented only by ice from going farther. The last land they saw lies below the 60th degree of latitude, not in the Southern Pacific, but Southern Atlantic Ocean, some 40 to 50° east of Cape Horn. They called it New Georgia and named one bay Forster's Bay and the most distant of the islands Southern Thule. They saw nothing but snow-clad mountains and valleys, above which lowered the most mournful sky they had ever seen; they observed, however, one darkish mountain. Some time previous to their reaching 71° 10′, they had already crossed the Antarctic Circle, but went back again. They saw the birds which are only to be found in the cold antarctic zone and are never met with elsewhere.

They twice searched for the Cap de la Circoncision which is marked on the charts, but never found it, so it probably does not exist. The large island discovered by them is Nova Caledonia, and is, I believe, below the 22° of latitude south, not far from New Holland: it is 80 English miles long. In the tract of country where Manicola is marked on Vaugondy's map they came across very intelligent creatures, whose faces, however, are more like apes than those of any other known people. They saw southern lights similar to our Aurora Borealis seven times, but only in the first year, and not when they were nearest the pole. He was accompanied by his twenty-one-year-old son, an excellent draughtsman; they discovered a large number of new species and families of animals and plants which they brought back with them, some in sketches and others in their natural state, not to mention other natural curiosities and products of the craftsmanship of the races they visited. They dealt in a truly wise and Christian manner with the poor devils, often withdrawing out of compassion if they showed any opposition. Once, however, when they needed water, and the savages, notwithstanding all their expostulations, attacked them and hurled a spear right through a sailor's cheeks, they had to shoot four of them before the rest would withdraw. Otaheiti and the neighbouring islands were more or less as Banks and Solander found them, though some things were changed. Notwithstanding Mr. Forster had not been robbed throughout his whole journey, even in Otaheiti, thieves broke into his house in London on the very first night after his return and stole many of his things; they were so kind, however, as to cast aside his books and manuscripts in a spot not far from his house. They were the true savages. You would scarce have believed, my dear Sir, that there are still savages in England, but I assure you I am not joking; I am referring to persons born in the fields, generally near the brick-kilns round London, of whom several are not baptized, still less circumcized. They grow up without learning to read or write, and never hear the words 'Religion' or 'Belief', and not even the word 'God', excepting in the phrase 'God damn it'. They gain their livelihood by all kinds of work in the brick-kilns, helping the drivers of hackney coaches, and so forth, until the old Adam in them is aroused; then they take to stealing and are generally hanged between the ages of 18 and 26. A short life and a merry one is their motto, which they do not hesitate to proclaim in court.

Mr. Forster's journey will not come out for a year; he himself will publish English and German editions. In the meantime, a sailor from his ship's crew is already having one printed and translated into German in London; it is full of inaccuracies and

intentional falsehoods. Mr. Forster, who knows the printer, has
taken pity on him and made several corrections both of the matter
and spelling. The voyage lasted three years and fourteen days.
They were exposed to dangers, though none of them particularly
great. Mr. Forster speaks of a voyage such as Anson's between
the tropics as I should of one to Holland, saying 'That was nothing
to signify, but that damned ice towards the South Pole was the
very devil!'—these were his very words. I asked him whether he
thought I could stand a voyage round the world. Then he looked
at me, asked me some questions, and said: 'Oh why shouldn't
you!' For this alone I like the man. Perhaps you have already
heard of the great utility of pickled cabbage and of mash, or beer
as it comes from malt; this discovery is in its way more important
than that of Harrison. It is thought here that the carbonic acid
which is swallowed with the vegetables, being absolutely necessary
for the maintenance of the body and present in large quantities
both in pickled cabbage and this beer, is the cause of this excellent
effect. What great things man will at length achieve with a
magnetic needle, a Harrison clock, and a load of pickled cabbage!
Thus far in Kew. The rest in London, for I must set off at once.

London, 17 October.
According to my promise I resume my letter, while eating my
breakfast in a coffee-house in which I have just spent the night.

Yesterday evening I saw Shakespeare's *As You Like It* played
at Drury Lane, being taken thereby the King's favourite page, and
before the play I was presented to Mr. Garrick (this is what I
really wished to tell you). So now I have not only seen this remarkable man in all his greatest parts, but also conversed with him.

Mr. Garrick brings me to Lavater's great work on Physiognomy.[1]
The Queen lent me the book, although she herself had only just
borrowed it. The paper, format, printing, and copper-plate
engravings, which are for the most part excellent, make an impression on one, even before one has read any of it, greatly to the
advantage of the observations themselves. Otherwise one is aware,

[1] *Physiognomische Fragmente zur Beförderung der Menschenkenntniss und
Menschenliebe*, first volume published at Leipzig in 1775.
Johann Kaspar Lavater, 1741–1801, pastor in Zürich, whose friendship with
Goethe was immortalized in the latter's poem: 'Zwischen Lavater und Basedow'.
Lavater's *Physiognomische Fragmente* enjoyed universal popularity, though
they were utterly unscientific, and thus unacceptable to Lichtenberg.

as in all the writings of this enthusiast, of a terrible plethora of
words, descriptions, and sensations, which do not lend themselves
to definition, and of observations, often indeed excellent, but
wrapped up in the jargon that is growing into fashion among the
so-called geniuses soaring in the clouds; so that any one looking for
facts rather than figures of speech loses patience a hundred times
over. Why does the fellow take so much pleasure in offering us
his Merseburg all froth and no body? Wilkes and Lord Lovat
are both copied after Hogarth in a masterly fashion, as, indeed,
is everything that Mr. Lavater has borrowed from Hogarth. The
copyist, notwithstanding his sparing use of lines in the drawing
of some of them, has lost nothing of the fire and nature in Hogarth's
work. But it is not very like Wilkes, and this, indeed, was not
Hogarth's intention in drawing him; Hogarth was known to be a
great antagonist of Churchill and Wilkes, and has portrayed the
former in the shape of a bear and the latter, as you will find him
in Lavater, as a caricature. Perhaps the hundred travelled barons
and shopmen who have seen Wilkes will say that it is as like him
as if he were looking at himself in a mirror. But this is not true.
Wilkes has small twinkling eyes, so that one scarcely notices that
he squints, and his side view has something most distinguished
and not at all disagreeable. Garrick's is much more like him;
except that he has uncommonly ardent, though small, eyes, and
in his whole demeanour something more agreeable than is expressed in the portrait.

Last Saturday evening when it was still light I spent two and
a half hours at Kew alone with the King and Queen. I had to tell
them about my journey. Later the two eldest Princesses and the
youngest Prince came in. I cannot describe to you, my dear Sir,
how lovely the Princesses have become; the Princess Royal is a
genuine beauty, and so are all the children. The King began to
write; he did not, however, dismiss me, but conversed with me
while doing so. Prince Adolphus asked for my stick, began to ride
on it, and pranced about so terribly among the cups and round the
writing-table that he had to hand over horse and stick to me again
with his own hands. As he came up to me, the Queen said, 'Now
say, I thank you, Sir,' which he spoke very clearly, bowing as he
did so. On the same day I talked with the Prince of Wales and
the Bishop in the garden at Richmond. The King showed me all
kinds of things which he had had made since he saw me last.

The cucumbers, for which I beg my most humble thanks, have arrived safely; I sent them, without opening them, to Lord Boston's country seat, where Mr. Irby is staying at present, and hope to taste them there.

I will not fail to obtain the Spa water for Herr Kriegs-Sekretär Glas. Dr. Priestley has hit upon some very fine subjects for investigation. In a preface to Hartley's[1] *Theory of the Human Mind* he acknowledges openly that he believes that man ceases entirely at death; in the *London Review*, written by Dr. Kenrick,[2] instead of contradicting him or warning the reader against him, they say: 'Some, indeed, will find this strange and too daring, but we believe that our thanks are due to Dr. Priestley for having had sufficient courage to make known to the world so important a truth.'

I was grieved to the heart by the quarrel between Hollmann and Kästner; Professors who play such a comedy for the benefit of their students of course lose their respect; and in my opinion they have little of this to lose, since in any case the student there imagines that he can act the Professor. Kästner wrote to me about the matter, sending me also three epigrams against Hollmann.

I shall probably set out on my journey homewards either on 30 October or 2 November. But I think I shall cross to Calais, in which case I should travel through Cassel to Göttingen. If I do so, perhaps I shall wait on you next Christmas in Hanover, my dear Sir.

LETTER 19

To DIETERICH

London, 18 October 1775.

My dear Dieterich,

Since Heaven is wise and just in all its purposes, I am always delighted when I can discover this wisdom and justice in such of its decrees as one generally submits to with reluctance. The death of your little daughter gave me this kind of philosophic comfort and led me to all manner of reflections which I will impart to you on some other occasion. I commiserate neither you nor her. She slept, ate pap, had plenty of kisses, I expect, and gave her parents unalloyed pleasure, thus both enjoying happiness and giving it.

---

[1] David Hartley, 1705–57, theologian and philosopher.
[2] William Kenrick, 1725–79, journalist, writer, and satirist.

It was, therefore, fitting that she should be taken. Those duties of a virtuous maiden which she could not fulfil will be undertaken in her stead by your other daughters, whom I hope that it may please Heaven to preserve until your image has again been reproduced. Therefore be content, my dear Dieterich, and go about your work, as I will do likewise, as soon as I have written a few more lines.

I spent last Saturday evening from 6 to 8 quite alone with both their Majesties. You can rest assured that I will further your interests whenever conditions are most favourable.

I shall set out either on 30 October or 3 November.

On the evening before last I was presented to Mr. Garrick by one of the King's pages. Afterwards I was taken to his box and in the company of his wife saw a play of Shakespeare represented. He paid me a great compliment which I may well repeat, since I take it at its face value. He said that he had never heard a foreigner speak English as I do, and that he would scarcely have taken me for one. Lately I passed through Stratford-on-Avon in Warwickshire, Shakespeare's birthplace. I saw his house and sat on his chair, from which people are beginning to cut away pieces. I made them cut me out some of it for one shilling. I shall have it made into rings and distribute them among the Jacobites and Goetheites[1] in the same way as the Lorenzo snuff-boxes.

The milliner's blocks for your Calendar are well engraved. I have found a man who will be responsible for it all for some slight remuneration. He is a man of proved honesty and exactness. I have spent 19 guineas on engravings for Gröningen, so it will be well worth the while of travellers to visit his house in Bremen.

I desire my best compliments to all my friends of both sexes. The carriage in which I am driving to Kew is already waiting at the door.

I received all the letters and packets quite safely.

Farewell. My eye is no longer inflamed, but is left in a condition which will sooner or later, I fear, deprive me of my sight.

G. C. Lichtenberg.

[1] Johann Georg Jacobi, 1740–1814, the poet, was so perfervid an admirer of Sterne that he presented snuff-boxes to his friends in memory of the Franciscan, Pater Lorenzo, who exchanges his as a token of amity with the traveller in the *Sentimental Journey*.

Lichtenberg apparently made up 'Goethiter' to pair with 'Jacobiter'. It would seem to refer to those who made a cult of Goethe's writings.

LETTER 20
To DIETERICH

London, 31 October 1775.

My dear Dieterich,

Well, yesterday morning I myself presented your petition to the King, as successfully as you could possibly wish. I must relate all to you in some detail, since it gives me just as great pleasure to write as you and all your true friends will have to read it. To begin with, however, I must confess something to you, about which I should for ever have kept silence, had not yesterday's opportunity come my way. That is to say, in the long conversation with the King a fortnight ago I let slip an opportunity of speaking of you (although not in the least through any fault of mine), which I could scarce expect to have again, but nevertheless chance offered me yesterday, when I made the best possible use of it. In that conversation I was telling the King of my journey and thus came at length to Madame Baskerville; when I mentioned this the King said, 'Perhaps many of the things you saw there will be of use to your friend Dieterich.' Scarcely had I uttered a few more words than a page came into the room with a locked box, which the King opened and, taking out some papers, began to write on them. Although I was not immediately dismissed, but conversed with the Queen for almost an hour longer at the other end of the room, and now and then with the King who, however, continued to sit at the writing-table, yet the thread of our conversation was broken off; it would have betrayed a lack of propriety, if not anything worse, had I turned the conversation again, and to have handed the King a petition while he was writing would have been utterly unthinkable. Little as I was to blame for this, I was, nevertheless, just as deeply grieved, and ascribed to remissness on my part what could by no means have been otherwise. Now, to proceed. Last Friday here in London I received a command through a page to wait on the King at 9 o'clock on the following Monday morning. I put your petition in my pocket and drove out there. The King was not alone. There was a large number of persons in the room, all standing, however, some distance off. Near the King stood Mr. Salgas, the first tutor of the Prince of Wales, and I. After addressing several questions to me, he at length inquired whether I knew what Counsellor Heyne was

engaged on at the moment. I said, 'No'. I hope, continued the
King, that in future Dieterich will print all his things, adding the
words (which he used of you once before), 'Dieterich is an
excellent fellow.' Now, thought I to myself, no mortal creature
shall rob me of this chance, even if the whole of Parliament were
in the room. So I began immediately to tell how their lordships
the Ministers honour your establishment with their approval,
that your printing-press is generally visited among the other
notable sights of Göttingen, and how greatly this establishment
deserved to be extended and patronized. The King was listening
to me with great attention when I came to the subject of your
petition, the whole of which I laid before him by word of mouth,
with observations of my own, adding then that I had it with me
in writing, upon which the King immediately held out his hand
for it. The packet being somewhat bulky, I told him that your
actual petition took up little space, while the rest contained the
necessary explanations, and the King said: 'Very good, very good,'
and, instead of giving it to the page in attendance on him, put the
whole bundle in his pocket. So now your affairs await the pleasure
of a King who has a very high opinion of you and is entirely pre-
possessed in favour of your establishment; and you ought, further,
so to contrive that the King is not advised against it from another
quarter. I assure you that I feel uncommonly light-hearted,
having executed your commission in such a manner that I couldn't
possibly have wished for a better. Some time later, about half an
hour after this, I had another conversation quite alone with him,
but the tenor of this, although I shall never forget it, is nothing to
the purpose here. I wanted to take leave of him. No, said the
King, we will see each other once more, and even left it open to
me as to whether this should be early on Thursday or Friday.[1]
I chose Friday, since the King is then in town. Now, dear
Dieterich, make a wise use of what I have told you here. It will
not be to your advantage to let many persons know of it; so tell
only those who needs must know, of whom there should be but
few. Show my letter to no one and do not confide in boon companions, who are indifferent as to whether things go well with you
or not. Be exact in all things, as far as possible, but especially in
matters which concern the University. The King is, I am firmly
convinced, both one of the most upright as well as one of the

[1] Because he knew that most of my time is now filled up.

most precise men I have ever seen. I assure you that you are in favour with him at present, and if you serve him with punctuality and zeal you cannot fail to experience the greatest benefit from this. Pray forgive a younger man for reading you such a sermon, because you are my friend.

Now, what is being done about a lodging? I shall be setting out from hence for certain on 6 November and, moreover, with three Englishmen, of whom one is a nephew of the Duke of Ancaster. They must all lodge under the same roof as me, even though it were the arsenal. So there must be at least four parlours and four bedrooms and an apartment in which one can breakfast and dine.[1] For Heaven's sake, don't leave me in the lurch, or I should have to move into the arsenal, forsooth. All through the winter I shall be looking out for a house which, please God, I can move into at Easter, if I don't occupy one near Ayrer's garden. I cough a great deal, am sleeping badly, and my eye does not mend, although I have led, and am leading, as regular an existence as a month-old lamb, excepting that I now and then drink a glass of wine instead of sheep's milk.

Last week I saw two tragedies on the same day of a vastly different kind. In the morning I saw them string up at Tyburn three footpads, a burglar, and a counterfeiter, and in the evening Mr. Garrick for the sixth time, in the part of Lusignan in *Zaïre*.

Of all the things that I (written with a big I) shall bring back, there will be nothing better in Göttingen than my legs, for I took them to London in a wretched state and yet have had little to complain of on their account.

I beg my kindest respects to your household and all my friends, and am

Your truly affectionate and faithful servant,

G. C. Lichtenberg.

The last time I shall write from England.
    (No written communication in answer to this.)

        2 November.

Since this letter had to wait for the quarterly courier, I have an opportunity of telling you of an incident which will certainly give you pleasure.

This morning at 10 o'clock the King visited me in my house.

[1] One servant's room, one only (Lichtenberg's note).

Heinrich, who saw him coming up to the door, ran towards it in the greatest confusion and opened it. The King inquired in German: 'Ist der Professor zu Hauss?' I threw my coat on in the other room, and, with stockings ungartered, and shoes looking like slippers, with the straps thrust underneath, I emerged and had a conversation with him which lasted for over a quarter of an hour. Did you ever hear anything like it?

LETTER 21

To DIETERICH

London, Sunday, 12 November 1775.

My dear Dieterich,

I write to you from London at a time when, a month ago, I thought to have been with you, or at least writing from Paderborn or Cassel. Two of the Englishmen who are coming with me were attacked by a bad epidemic cold, of which many people have died, and which I also had, though without fever. I believe and hope that a week to-morrow we shall be fit to set out. Take care to provide us with good lodgings and beds. Mattresses, of course, but no feather coverlets, God forbid! Covers of waste paper would be better.

On the last day I was with the King I spent three hours with him, and as I took my departure he said all manner of things to me which I shall never forget. He presented me with several books and 1,200 thalers: it is regarded as a special mark of favour and condescension that he did not have it paid out to me, but gave it to me with his own hands. Don't say a word to any one. More by word of mouth. I do not return willingly to Göttingen and scarce think that I shall ever be able to live there contentedly. Farewell, and pray remember me most kindly to all my friends.

G. C. Lichtenberg.

Yesterday evening I heard the famous Gabrielli sing in the opera *Didone Abbandonata*. Read to Christelchen, or make her read for herself, the description given of her by Brydone in the second part of his *Tour through Sicily and Malta*.

I lately saw Garrick play again, which makes seven times altogether.

I should much like to bring something for little Wilhelm, Luisgen, and Frederickchen, if it were not for the damned customs officers at the coast. The rascals confiscate everything which has not been worn or used, and, begad, I can hardly wear a gown, or a Hussar's sword, or say that I myself have used a toy horse with a whistle behind.

If you see Mr. Dohm pray tell him that I desire my humble respects to him and that I have received his letter. Also that Mr. Planta[1] will do everything that I could not do myself; the rest of his questions I shall soon answer in person.

I send you herewith some prints of almanacs, merely in order to show you how early you can in future obtain them. These are the very first. I have had them in the house for about a week, and the others do not come out until nearly December. For the most part they are badly drawn, especially the faces; indeed, English dairymaids have better.

The feathers are far too modest. Only yesterday evening I saw the Duchess of Devonshire, who is here portrayed dancing, adorned thus at the Opera. I assure you that this is no exaggeration; a single such feather costs a guinea; they are red, white, and black.[2]

LETTER 22

To DIETERICH

London, 16 November 1775.

My dear Dieterich,

Once again I am writing to you, and even request an answer of you. I shall not set out until the first week in December and hope therefore that, if you sit down and write immediately, your letter will still find me here. I again kept my room for three days, which would be nothing in Göttingen, but in London is a veritable affliction for a heart-whole man about to take his departure.

Pray ask Professor Büttner[3] immediately whether I shall buy

[1] Joseph Planta, 1744–1827, Assistant Librarian at the British Museum, F.R.S., Keeper of MSS., Principal Librarian 1799–1827.

[2] At the end of the letter in the 1901 edition is a drawing of the head of a lady—presumably the Duchess of Devonshire—with an enormous head-dress of feathers.

[3] See note, p. 87.

him an Irish–English Dictionary on which I chanced. It is in
4to and printed in Paris in 1732. At the end is an Irish Grammar;
this is the part with the English first. The anonymous compiler
announces in the preface another part with the Irish first. They
tell me, however, that this has never appeared. The man wants
half a guinea for it. I was unable to procure an Irish and Gaelic
Bible, but I did purchase one in the Welsh tongue for the Professor,
though I had to pay 9 shillings for it. Pray tell Herr Blumenbach[1]
that I beg leave to present my humble respects to him and that
I will do all in my power to oblige him as regards most of his
inquiries; I have everywhere extolled his industry. Mr. Aiton, the
botanic gardener at Kew, will be delighted not only to correspond
with him, but to procure everything for him, as far as lies in his
power. I am now living by myself in a coffee-house, while Heinrich is in Lord Boston's house a mile away. Next Monday I shall
go into the country again. There are a great many deaths here at
present, and several persons who have more to lose than your
friend are excessively anxious. I keep quite calm and go on leading
as regular an existence as before, without taking any greater care
of myself. If I die, I shall not go back to Germany, that's all.

I only wish that you could see for once a London day like this
one: it is pouring as though the angels thought that there was a
conflagration down here, and my street is enveloped in so thick
a cloud of coal smoke that, in order not to harm my eyes, I am
writing by the light of a candle (at half-past ten in the morning);
and yet at ten o'clock yesterday night it was starlight and freezing
hard. One could certainly not endure it were it not for other
consolations which far outweigh all that. In a word (between you
and me), if it were not for the inconceivably lovely, obliging, naïve
creatures, ready to be helpful on every occasion, who warm one's
bed, I would wager that all the Englishmen would quit England,
at least for the winter.

Farewell, my dear friend; I desire to be most kindly remembered
to your household and that of Baldinger.

G. C. Lichtenberg.

[1] Johann Friedrich Blumenbach, 1752–1840, Professor of Medicine at
Göttingen and a pioneer in the study of Anthropology.

LETTER 23

To DIETERICH

London, 1 December 1775.

My dear Dieterich,

I write to you yet once again from London, and then no more for the present. It is two nephews (not brothers) of the Duke of Ancaster whom I am bringing with me, and the third is another very young man; the eldest of them is not yet 16, but almost all of them are considerably taller than you. Unless anything unforeseen occurs, we shall set out from hence next Thursday, 7 December. We shall probably travel through Cassel, where we intend to rest; how would it be if you sent your coach with post-horses to Münden for us? But I will write further about this from Cassel. Next Sunday week I shall be going on board the ship and entrusting myself to the sea, which this year is even more unkind than usual. In the stretch between Amsterdam and Scheveningen alone as many as thirty rudders have been found; so thirty ships have been wrecked near there, since each ship has only one rudder. On 14 November during one of these storms a melancholy event occurred. Major Caulfield,[1] a member of the Irish parliament, was travelling from this country to Ireland with his wife, a grown-up daughter, one or two small children, a cousin, all his servants, and a large sum of money. When he reached Parkgate, where he wished to take the packet, the Captain told him that, to judge by the clouds, it was blowing up for a storm and he should not sail that night. The Major entreated him most earnestly, protesting that the crossing was short and that they should be in Ireland before the storm, which he apprehended, broke. The Major himself went to the inns in the place where the travellers who had taken their passage on the ship were lodging, got them all together, and persuaded them. At length the Captain gave way and they set sail at eleven o'clock at night. Scarcely had they been gone half an hour than a contrary wind arose and drove them back into the harbour. Some time later the Captain again attempted to put out

---

[1] The Hon. Francis Caulfield, second son of the third Viscount Charlemont and brother of the first earl of Charlemont. In 1760 he married Mary, daughter of John, Lord Eyre, M.P. for Charlemont. He was drowned with his wife and infant daughter on 19 October 1775, not on 14 November, as Lichtenberg states. See *Gent. Mag.* xlv. 548.

to sea, but for the second time he was forced to make for the harbour. They waited for some time and had almost decided to remain there, when a wind arose which was at least blowing in the right direction, and so they put out to sea. The same wind became a storm, and no more has ever been heard either of the large number of persons on board or of the ship itself. They say that the wife and daughter were excellent persons, both beautiful and virtuous. They have a son still at school here in London and a daughter in Ireland. Another ship came so near them in the dark that the sailors could hear the cries of distress and screams of the persons on the ship, but were unable to help them. Another packet-boat which put out to sea at the same time was also lost. The storm here in London was so violent that I was in half a mind to go out into the street, fearing lest the house should fall in, which is no rare occurrence in London.

I send you herewith some more fashion plates. There's no keeping up with them, for each lady dresses herself as her whim prompts her, and every whore as the devil does. The two sheets which I have marked on the back with noughts are 'Ladies of the town', or common W——s, as they go about the streets of an evening; in the public places they are dressed with as great magnificence as a female form can possibly display.

Pray see to the lodgings. I should be delighted to bring some hats with me, if the old devils in Harwich were not so strict, and were hats easier to pack; they are very cumbersome, and without them I have two large boxes crammed full of engravings, books, and trumpery, English and German. I have had five entire suits made in England, not indeed out of vanity, but for sheer need of a covering, and I am taking them all with me.

Farewell. I beg my respects to my good friends of both sexes.

G. C. Lichtenberg.

God willing, I shall dine with you on Christmas Eve. If you will have something good served up, I will tell you many a good tale, if my eye is well.

I have just read a circumstantial account of Mr. Caulfield's disaster. He is not a major, but a baronet of large fortune. The rudders were found between Helvoetsluys and Scheveningen. There were twenty-six of them.

DIARY

Note: Lichtenberg was twice in England, first in 1770, and then in 1774 into 1775. This first fragment deals with his first journey—the rest deal with the second.

FIRST JOURNEY.

On Saturday, 7 April, we came to Helvoetsluys, where we put up at the Golden Lion. This place is made most agreeable and lively by the great number of sailors who are constantly walking up and down the streets. When there is a moderately high sea its roaring can be heard at the inn. I discovered here how sea-water tasted. Owing to adverse winds the English packet-boat had already been several days in the harbour; at twelve o'clock midday the weather cleared and the wind seemed to be turning rather to our advantage. It was therefore agreed that we should go on board at ten o'clock in the evening and make sail at one o'clock. During a short walk down to the sea, which I took in the evening by moonlight, the colour of the moon did not predict the best weather, and much trouble might have been saved if only the captain had consulted a barometer.

We made a good supper and went cheerfully on board about half-past ten on the night before Palm Sunday. The Captain, whose name was Story, was an agreeable man and an expert sailor, having made the voyage to America several times. Among our travelling companions was a Captain Douglas, a man of much wisdom and experience, who had helped to conquer America and had conducted the English mathematicians to the North Cape, where they wished to observe the transit of Venus. His company was a genuine comfort to us.

At about ten o'clock in the morning I was overcome by my first attack of sea-sickness, which affliction lasted until five o'clock in the afternoon. It is not a very agreeable condition, though not so bad as people sometimes make it out to be; or perhaps this illness did not seize upon me as it did upon others in the ship who evidently thought themselves dying. For my part I suffered greater discomfort from the storm, which brought rain, hail, and snow and put the ship into such a motion that great cases were pitched from one side to another, making a crashing din, so that it seemed as if the ship must go to pieces. The Captain himself was once with great violence thrown on to the deck; and a wave rolled into my bed, so that I had to change over into another; this was a very slow process owing to the great rolling of the ship, which made it almost impossible to move. At last our foresail ripped to pieces, and all the sailors except two or three were sick. So now there was nothing to be done but to steer for deep water and, moreover, to put Harwich out of our mind for the time being.

We drifted hither and thither until day broke and the wind turned to our advantage, so that in sixteen hours we made good our loss and, notwithstanding we had gone as far as Yarmouth, cast anchor at Harwich after ten o'clock on the evening of 9 April.

The custom-house officers came on board the ship and searched our pockets and among our clothes with excessive roughness. In order to leave the ship we were forced, at peril of life and limb, in rain and wind and great waves, to climb down into a small boat, which took us to the land in a quarter of an hour. The moment one sets foot in England one is struck by the speed, willingness, and propriety with which all one's desires are fulfilled and by the number of handsome girls. Even the lowest are such pretty little creatures that any one who is not quite sure of himself in this respect had best keep away from England. Their charms are enhanced, moreover, by their costume, which would set off a German charwoman.

From Harwich to London the distance is 74 miles. The road is excellent, and at every mile stands a stone on which the distance to London is marked. The postilions drive with such speed that it gives one a singing in the ears, and with eyes and hands so intent on their occupation that one might almost believe these men to be gentlemen of quality, who had to-day been taken with the whim of playing postilion in the service of some of their friends. The places where we changed horses were Colchester and Ingatestone. The first place is of considerable size and is full of small shops. Its oysters are famous throughout England, and at the proper season are daily consumed at the tables of the great. The shell is thin and scarcely half as large as those which we know at home; but the oyster fills up the whole of it and is larger than the common oyster. Near Ingatestone we passed through a village where a fair was being held, and, as the postilion pulled up, our coach was immediately surrounded by more than a hundred children who laughed at us, pointing now at one and now at another and saying,

'Look, there is a bullock.' But I do not know how it is; there is about these people a kind of good-natured roughness, very different from the roughness of my native land, where the mob, indeed, pays less attention to strangers than it does in England, but when once they have taken it into their heads to do so there is no escaping them.

I arrived in London at about half-past ten on the night of 10 April, but did not reach Lord Boston's house until twelve. Nevertheless, the noise in the streets was as great as in other places at midday. This is not surprising, when you think that 11 p.m. or half-past is the regular supper-time in many genteel families, and also that at that hour in this famous commercial city they begin to ply those kinds of trade which could not proceed during the day.

SECOND JOURNEY.

I set out from Göttingen on Monday, 29 August 1774, at 11 o'clock in the morning, and set foot on land in Essex on 25 September at 3 o'clock in the afternoon, after a sea-voyage of twenty-four hours. On 27 September I reached London and was set down in Oxford Street.

At Drury Lane I saw *The Fair Quaker*, as well as *The Elopement* and *The Naval Review*. Mr. Moody was Commodore Flip and played his part excellently; in other respects the play did not appear to me to be the work of a master-hand. Mr. Weston, in the part of a sailor, was very droll. Sir Francis, who had himself been present on that occasion, assured me that the presentation of the naval review was very good. Nothing pleased me so much as the song, 'Britannia rules the Main', &c.; there is something really great about it. Many persons in the gallery joined in, producing a splendid effect. *The Elopement* is a pantomime, staged with excessive magnificence, in which Harlequin plays all manner of characteristic tricks; the scenery is wonderful.

Bunbury,[1] a man of large fortune, has a great gift for seizing on the ludicrous in the human form, and of drawing caricatures with great taste on the spur of the moment. His skill is incredible.

[1] Henry William Bunbury, 1750–1811, caricaturist and artist, chiefly drew in pencil and chalk, a close friend of Reynolds, Goldsmith, and Garrick.

They say that sometimes, when he has observed anything, on returning home he springs out of his carriage, runs into his house, and even before his wife, who is following, can enter the room, he has already made a sketch of everything.

At the races at Epsom £50,000 were gambled away. Six thousand guineas were offered for the winning horse.

Many years ago a foolish fellow in the Lifeguards said that on a certain day, which he named, London would be destroyed by an earthquake. Great numbers of the inhabitants were filled with such terror by this that almost all the boats on the Thames were hired for that day, so that the people could escape in them at the beginning of the earthquake. For this purpose they waited near the stairs. The late Prince of Wales, who was at that time staying in the country at Clifden, came to town on purpose to set an example of courage to the populace; but all in vain.

The second play was an operetta, *The Cobbler, or a Wife of Ten Thousand*. This piece is new, and the music is by Dibdin.[1] On the evening when I was present it was hissed off the stage. A greater din than was then made cannot be imagined: one section hissed, another applauded, one yelling 'Go on, go on, on, on, on,' and the other just as vociferously, 'Off, off, off.' As you can well imagine, the Off's were bound to conquer the On's, since, though the On's could make just as much noise as the Off's, the latter were able to carry the day by keeping on longer. After I had commiserated the poor actors, who stood there not knowing what to do for more than a quarter of an hour, Mr. Dibdin at last bowed to the audience, and the curtain fell. This was the only play among all those I have seen which was not played through. On the following day Mr. Garrick presented it again, to every one's surprise; this time it met with approval, and to-day, as I write, it is being given again.

On 25 February, which was like a summer day, I went for a walk with Mr. Irby in Kensington Gardens. On the way he pointed out to me a small chapel, some distance off, and said:

[1] Charles Dibdin, 1745–1814, play-writer and song-writer. This play caused riots, a notorious episode in theatrical life.

'That is the churchyard in which Sterne is buried.' We went there together. An old woman showed us his grave; it is marked by a miserable stone which was put up to him by two freemasons, W. and S. The inscription in verse on it might be better. Perhaps this wretched stone will some day serve to point out to some rich man of sensibility the spot on which he might place a more worthy monument. The grave lies, I may add, hardly a gun-shot from the place where criminals are executed (Tyburn).

Mr. de Grey[1] told me that Yorick was a very tiresome visitor. He would frequently wait on people at 9 o'clock in the morning and scarcely ever leave before 9 o'clock in the evening. When they went out he went with them and then came back with them. He was very poor.

On 7 March a club, which used to meet on Tuesdays in Wych Street, was dissolved. It consisted of servants, journeymen, and apprentices. On these evenings every member laid down four-pence, for which he had music and a female gratis; anything else had to be paid for separately. Twenty of the girls were brought before Sir John Fielding;[2] the beauty of some of them aroused general admiration.

On 19 March I went walking with Mr. Burrows to Newington Green; he pointed out to me an inn with a small covered balcony, where on a summer afternoon they sometimes serve two pipes, that is to say, 240 gallons, of tea.

On the 15th I dined in the company of General Paoli with Herr von Alvensleben.[3] Paoli is a very handsome man of the most exquisite breeding. He has not a martial appearance; in fact, the expression of his eyes is gentle, and one would not easily take him for a man who had for so long been the leader of a war-like people. One would be more inclined to think that he had

---

[1] Lichtenberg probably refers to the son of the first Baron Walsingham, who died 9 May 1781. See Wm. Irby's letter to Lichtenberg 30 September 1781: 'De Grey is become a Peer by the death of his Father.' Hecht: *Briefe aus Lichtenbergs englischem Freundeskreis*, 1925, p. 36.

[2] Fielding, died 1780, the noted blind Bow Street magistrate.

[3] Privy-Councillor in Hanover and at that period of the reign of George III chief of the German Chancery in London.

grown up at the card-table. He is an excellent talker and made
some very apt comparisons between Rome and Sparta; he expressed the opinion that the English would be made more warlike
by their merchants; a vastly strange notion.

On the 24th I was introduced to Mr. Solander[1] at the Museum;
he was accompanied by the man from Ulietea, Omai, with whom
I had some conversation. He took my hand and shook it in the
English fashion. He is a well-grown man and has not the un-
pleasantly marked features of the negro; his colour is a yellowish
brown. I asked him whether he liked England better than his
native country, and he said 'yes'. He cannot pronounce 'yes' and
it sounded almost like 'vis'. I made him say the English 'th',
which he could do fairly well. In answer to the question how the
winter in England suited him, he said 'Cold, cold', shaking his
head. Wishing to explain that in his native country no shirt, or
at least a very thin one, was worn, he seized the ruffle of his linen
shirt and pulled the waistcoat away from it. His English is very
indistinct, and without Mr. Planta's help, I really believe that I
could have followed nothing of it. There is in his demeanour
something very pleasant and unassuming which is most suitable,
and of which no African face is capable. His hands are marked
with blue stains which form circles round the fingers of his right
hand; pointing to them, he said 'Wives', and to those on his left
hand, 'Friends'. This was all the speech I was able to have with
him on this day, the company being very numerous, and both of
us somewhat bashful. It was far from being disagreeable to me to
see my right hand clasped by another, hailing from the opposite
end of the earth.

On the 25th I breakfasted with Mr. Solander and Omai in
Banks's[2] room. Mr. Banks had gone hunting. Omai was put next
to me and was very lively. As soon as he had saluted us all he
sat down at the tea-table and made the tea with great propriety. I

[1] Daniel Charles Solander, the celebrated botanist, 1736–82, a native of
Sweden, a pupil of Linné. He came to England in 1760, was appointed to a
professorship at St. Petersburg University, but did not take it up. For a time
he was an assistant in the British Museum. In 1768 he went with Joseph Banks
on Cook's voyage in the *Endeavour* and went later with Banks to Ireland. He
was appointed in 1773 to be Keeper of the Natural History Department of the
British Museum.

[2] Sir Joseph Banks, 1743–1820, the famous naturalist, who accompanied
Cook on his first voyage of discovery. President of the Royal Society of Science
in London.

induced him to pronounce the name of his island, and it sounded almost like 'Ulieta-je'. He cannot pronounce any *s*, at least, not at the beginning of a word. He pronounces 'Solander' like 'Tolando'. I asked him whether his father and mother were still living; and he turned up his eyes, then shut them, leaning his head on one side, to explain that they were both dead. When I asked after his brothers and sisters he first held up two fingers, saying 'ladies', then three fingers, saying 'men', by which he wished to indicate that he had two sisters and three brothers. He appears to have little curiosity: though wearing a watch, he does not concern himself much about the way it works. While we were looking at the beautiful drawings of the island Pomona and other islands, he sat down by the fireplace and went to sleep. It is very doubtful whether he will become a Czar Peter for his nation, although he undertook this journey to give himself consequence. He was vastly delighted with Sadler's Wells[1] and needs must go there again the very next day; after this, however, he became indifferent to it. He plays chess. At breakfast he ate no pastry, but only a little salted salmon, which was almost raw. I tasted some of it, and felt so much indisposed that even now, six hours later, I am scarce recovered.

Mr. Solander told us that he went on Omai's arrival to the coffee-house where he and Captain Fourneaux then were; but before he had entered the room in which Omai was, the latter had already recognized his voice and, calling out 'There is Tolando!' was about to go up to him. He did not, however, recognize Solander's face, probably on account of the difference in his costume and appearance, so he called out several times, 'Tolando, speak, speak!' As soon as Solander had spoken he immediately ran towards him. He knew Mr. Banks at once, although neither Banks nor Solander remember ever having seen him on his island. His teeth are exquisitely white, regular, and close.

On 15 April, the Saturday before Easter, I went walking in Hyde Park in the evening after tea. The full moon had just risen and was shining over Westminster Abbey. The solemnity of the eve of such a day moved me to indulge in my favourite reflections

---

[1] One of the smaller London theatres. Its chief distinction at that time was in having the whole space beneath the stage filled with water, which made it especially suitable for representing aquatic scenes.

with voluptuous melancholy. I sauntered along Piccadilly and
down the Haymarket to Whitehall, both in order to look again on
the statue of Charles the First against the bright western sky and
to give myself up in the moonlight to my own reflections on the
Banqueting Hall, the house through the window of which
Charles I walked out on to the scaffold. Here I chanced to meet
one of those persons who hire organs, which often cost as much
as £40 or £50, from the organ-makers, and haunt the streets night
and day, playing as they go, until some one calls them and gives
them sixpence to play through their piece. The organ was good,
and I followed him slowly along the pavement, while he was
walking in the middle of the street. Suddenly he began to play
the wonderful chorale: 'In allen meinen Taten' ('In all my
deeds'),[1] with such melancholy, well attuned to my earlier mood,
that I was seized with an indescribable sense of pious awe. I
thought of my distant friends, my sorrows became endurable
and vanished entirely. We had gone some two hundred paces
beyond the Banqueting Hall when I called the fellow, and, leading
him nearer to the house, made him play that magnificent hymn.
I could not refrain from singing the words quietly to myself:

> 'Hast du es denn beschlossen,
> So will ich unverdrossen
> An mein Verhängnis gehen.'

('If Thou hast ordained it, I will meet my fate undismayed.')
Before me lay the majestic building, lit up by the full moon: it
was Easter Eve; and from this window Charles came forth to
exchange a corruptible crown for an incorruptible. O God, what
is the greatness of this world!

Wrest[2] is the seat of the former Dukes of Kent. Lord Hard-
wycke[3] married the heiress and is owner of the estate, but has

[1]   'In allen meinen Taten
         Lass' ich den Höchsten raten,
         Der alles kann und hat',
beginning of the famous hymn written by Paul Fleming (1609-40) on his
journey to Persia in 1633. See *Oxford Book of German Verse*, No. 35.

[2] Wrest Park, ten miles south of Bedford, was the estate of the family of Grey
of Ruthin. Henry de Grey was created Duke of Kent in 1710, but that title died
out in 1740. He made the gardens, guided by Lancelot Browne. Flitton is about
three miles distant. It has a perpendicular church with the Grey mausoleum, a
number of effigies and brasses.

[3] A reference apparently to Philip, second earl of Hardwicke, 1720-90,
eldest son of Lord Chancellor Hardwicke.

permitted Lord Polwarth,[1] his son-in-law, to have the use of it.
Garden and park, which were laid out by Browne, are enchanting.
The prospect from the house on to the hill is open and beautiful;
otherwise the house and garden are somewhat low-lying. The
lack of a wide prospect in the garden is more than compensated
for by the pleasant lawns near-by, the varied shrubs, the pavilion
and obelisk, the herds of deer which roam about among the trees
planted here and there, the handsome exterior of the house, and
many other charming objects. In the house is an excellent library,
consisting for the most part of historical books, books of travel,
and architectural works. Two miles from Wrest, at Flitton, is the
family burial-place of the Dukes, where there is a very fine monument over the vault of the Duke and his wife.

I myself have heard some one advocate quite dispassionately
the rights of the Americans; he said, 'I believe this, it is indeed
my opinion; but, as I receive £600 a year from the Court, I have
to *speak* differently.' Every one, perhaps, thinks thus. Luxury
and extravagance have risen to such a pitch as never before in the
history of the world; the saddest of all, as Dr. Price[2] remarked, is
that the very luxury which, on the one hand, is the ruin of the
country, on the other is its support. Tickets for masked balls
have been issued, for which the drawings cost 50 guineas. Thus
the entrance ticket for a masquerade at the Pantheon was designed
by Cypriani[3] and engraved by Bartolozzi.[4]

The Englishman cooks his soups in his stomach, so that he
may be sure that their strength does not evaporate.

[1] Alexander, Lord Polwarth, son of the third earl of Marchmont; he married
the eldest daughter of Philip, second earl of Hardwicke. In 1776 he was made
a peer of the United Kingdom with the title of Baron Hume of Berwick. The
British title became extinct in 1781.

[2] Richard Price, writer on political economy, 1723–91.

[3] Giovanni Battista Cipriani, Italian painter and engraver, who enjoyed a
great reputation in England.

[4] Francesco Bartolozzi, 1730–1815, one of the most famous copperplate
engravers.

APPENDIX

The 'Deutsches Museum' and its Place among German Literary Periodicals in the Eighteenth Century

IN the eighteenth century literary work was even worse paid in Germany than in England. Authors received, moreover, little encouragement from the wealthier members of society on account of the low standard of education of the majority of the nobles and the prevalence of the taste for French literature among the cultured. The most remunerative means of earning a living by one's pen was to write for one of the many literary magazines, which enjoyed a wide, though sometimes short-lived, popularity. These were for the most part modelled on the English *Tatler*, *Spectator*, and *Guardian*. Perhaps few of the German magazines of the eighteenth century have as much literary merit as their famous English prototypes. They had, however, an even wider influence, being read not only by the leisured classes but by the people as a whole, so that they contributed in no small measure towards the re-awakening of German literature during the latter half of the century.

The first of these periodicals was *Der Vernünfftler*, which appeared in Hamburg in 1713. The popularity of such publications increased yearly, so that by the end of the eighteenth century more than five hundred of them were published in Germany. It is impossible here to name more than a few of them. Those which have the greatest interest for posterity are such as were used as a vehicle for the expression of the views of some particular school or author, as, for instance, the *Discourse der Mahler* (1721) of Bodmer and Breitinger, Gottsched's *Die vernünftigen Tadlerinnen* (1725) and *Beyträge zur critischen Historie der deutschen Sprache* (1732–44), and the famous *Bremer Beyträge* (1744–8) which challenged Gottsched's views. With *Briefe die neueste Literatur betreffend* (1759–65) and the *Hamburgische Dramaturgie* (1767–8) we come to a landmark in literary criticism. In them Lessing, whom Macaulay called 'the first critic in Europe', laid the foundation of all modern criticism. One of the most successful periodicals of the day was Wieland's *Der Teutsche Merkur* (1773–89). The two greatest poets of the century included the editing of such works in their manifold activities, and we have Schiller's *Rheinische Thalia* (1785–93) and *Die Horen* (1795–7), to which Goethe contributed largely, and Goethe's *Prophyläen*.

Lichtenberg did his share of work for popular magazines, largely on account of his friendship with Dieterich, the printer and publisher. From 1778 until 1799 Lichtenberg edited for him the *Göttinger Taschenkalender*, where fashion notes are to be found beside literary articles and polemical writings. The *Göttingisches Magazin der Wissenschaften und Literatur* (1780–5), which Lichtenberg edited jointly with Georg Forster, is more serious and scientific in its tone, and therefore appealed to a more limited public.

We are here concerned with Lichtenberg's connexion with Boie, one of the most successful of all the many editors of periodicals of his day. With Boie's earlier venture, made jointly with Gotter, the famous *Göttinger Musenalmanach* (1770–1802), Lichtenberg had no great sympathy (see Letter 9, PS. 2, and Letter 10). This magazine has a great interest for students of German literature, being the chosen organ for the publication of the work of that group of poets known as the 'Göttinger Hainbund' (see note, p. 71). Lichtenberg held in much higher esteem the *Deutsches Museum*, where the three so-called *Briefe aus England*, which are here translated into English, appeared in the numbers of 1776–8. Articles in the form of letters were a favourite literary device of the period both in English and German magazines. They were often addressed to some imaginary recipient, such as the fictitious officer of Lessing's *Literaturbriefe*. We must not, however, be misled by the fact of Lichtenberg's acquaintance with Boie into thinking of the 'Letters from England' as personal letters. They were obviously compiled with care, with a view to publication, from the copious notes made by Lichtenberg in his Diary (cf. *Jahrbuch der deutschen Shakespeare-Gesellschaft*, 42sten Jahrgang, 1906, *Notizen über die englische Bühne aus Lichtenbergs Tagebüchern*, mitgeteilt von Albert Leitzmann).

The first number of the *Deutsches Museum*, edited by Boie and Dohm, appeared in January 1776. They gave as their object: 'die Deutschen mit sich selbst bekannter und auf ihre eignen Nationalangelegenheiten aufmerksamer zu machen', and did their best to further it by publishing articles on the state of literature, politics, and manufactures in all parts of Germany, as well as a limited number of poems. Boie had become tired of the spate of poems by second-rate authors that had flowed into the *Musenalmanach*, and was glad to turn to work of a more solid and intellectual nature. From 1776 to 1788 the magazine was published twice yearly by the Weygandsche Buchhandlung of Leipzig, and from 1789 to 1791, under Boie's sole editorship and the name of *Neues Deutsches Museum*, by Georg Joachim Göschen. It was one of the most influential periodicals of the day, and Lichtenberg's articles on the English stage were widely read and discussed. His further connexion with the *Deutsches Museum* was not so happy, for in it appeared the writings of J. H. Voss in the acrimonious controversy he entered into with Lichtenberg and C. G. Heyne. Boie was so greatly displeased at the anger aroused against himself, as editor, as well as against the offending Voss, in Göttingen circles, that he threatened to give up editing the paper.

SELECT BIBLIOGRAPHY

LICHTENBERG, GEORG CHRISTOPH. *Vermischte Schriften*. Göttingen, 1844–6. *Briefe*, edited A. Leitzmann u. C. Schüddekopf, Leipzig, 1901–2.

BOUILLIER, VICTOR. *Georg Christoph Lichtenberg. Essai sur sa vie et ses œuvres*. Paris, 1914.

BRUFORD, WALTER HORACE. *Germany in the XVIII Century*. Cambridge, 1935.

HECHT, HANS. *Briefe aus Lichtenbergs englischem Freundeskreis*, edited by H. Hecht. Göttingen, 1925.

HENTZSCHEL, OTTO. *Lichtenbergs Lebensanschauung*. Diss. Leipzig, 1910.

KLEINEIBST, RICHARD. *G. Ch. Lichtenbergs Stellung zur deutschen Literatur*. Strassburg, 1915.

SCHAEFER, FRIEDRICH. *Georg Christoph Lichtenberg als Psychologe und Menschenkenner*. Jena, 1898.

INDEX